Grandma Was a Kitchen Healer and Grandpa Grew Roses

A Collection of Short Stories
Life : The Good, the Bad, and the Amusing

Jim Great Elk Waters
Kelly V. Pavlovic

Grandma Was a Kitchen Healer and Grandpa Grew Roses

A Collection of Short Stories
Life : The Good, the Bad, and the Amusing

by Jim Great Elk Waters
Kelly V. Pavlovic

Publishing Division

Grandma Was a Kitchen Healer and Grandpa Grew Roses
Life: The Good, the Bad, and the Amusing
A Collection of Short Stories

© Copyright 2020 by The WeWán Institute. All rights reserved.

No part of this publication may be reproduced, distributed, or transmitted in any form or by any means, including photocopying, recording, or other electronic or mechanical methods, or by any information storage and retrieval system, without prior written permission from the publisher, except for brief quotations embodied in critical reviews and certain other noncommercial uses permitted by copyright law. For permission requests, write to the publisher at the address below:

ATTN: Permissions Coordinator "Grandma Was a Kitchen Healer"
The WeWán Institute
thekeepers@wewan.org
www.wewan.org

First Edition: December 2020
Printed in the United States of America
ISBN 978-1-7361647-0-9

Disclaimer: Although the authors and publisher have made every effort to ensure that the information in this book was correct at press time, the authors and publisher do not assume and hereby disclaim any liability to any party for any loss, damage, or disruption caused by similarities, errors or omissions, whether such similarities, errors or omissions result from negligence, accident, or any other cause.

6"x9" Paperback
Typeface: Californian FB
Software: Pages 2020, Adobe Photoshop 2021
Cover Design & Interior Design: The WeWán Institute Design Team

All photographs appearing in this book are the property of the The WeWán Institute. They are protected by U.S. Copyright Laws, and are not to be reproduced in any way without the written permission of The WeWán Institute.
© Copyright 2020 The WeWán Institute, All Rights Reserved.

PRAISE FOR...
"Grandma Was a Kitchen Healer and Grandpa Grew Roses"

Who can resist a title like "Grandma Was a Kitchen Healer and Grandpa Grew Roses?" I would liken this book to sitting around a battered old kitchen table with friends and endless cups of coffee, swapping stories and then having those stories stir long dormant memories of your own history. More than once, I would look up from the page and remember my own Grandma's and Mom's home remedies or my Dad teaching me the value of hard work and tenacity by assigning me real chores. The authors take turns with chapters and sharing tales of family and events that shaped their lives and each has a distinctive voice – Jim Great Elk Waters has the gravitas of an elder and worldly experience; Kelly Pavlovic's voice is lighter and quicker, and she freely shares how life events and times of inner turmoil have shaped her. Despite how unique each of our histories are, there is a commonality that links every family's story, and the authors reminded me of that by sharing themselves and their families. I would recommend this as a "night table" book – meaning it's one that you'll want to keep close by to dip in again and again.

- Darlene Southern
Cave Creek, AZ
Carefree Property Services

This book is nothing short of a treasure. Waters and Pavlovic offer a humble collection of stories from their lifetimes and those of their Ancestors. This is their legacy. Their ancestors speak great wisdom through them, passing down the treasured stories that are as relevant today as they were before our feet touched the ground. This book will give you the courage you need to discover the magic and the gift of life. This book will inspire you, as it has me.

- Dianne Hellrigel
Los Angeles, CA
E.D. and V.P. of the St. Francis Dam National Memorial

"Grandma Was a Kitchen Healer" is better than a great read, it's a life enhancing read. This book will change your life – story by story. Through the telling of the authors' family stories, they enable the reader to recall one's own history –experiencing them again in vivid living color – and inspires the retelling to generations to come. One thing better than the stories told by Jim and Kelly are knowing them personally and having the honor to hear some of these stories from their own lips, in their own voices. They interweave themselves into the very fabric of your tapestry. Reading this book will begin a domino effect in you that will be endlessly inspiring. As Jim and Kelly say, "Everyone has a story…" and it's one that absolutely needs to be told, heard, and experienced. Be selfish: READ THIS BOOK – and give yourself the pleasure that'll make your heart shout what your mouth will never be able to whisper and your soul will never forget.

- Chuck Behrens
Bay Village, OH
Motivational Speaker and author of "The Candle Maker"

Can't express how much I enjoyed the book. I laughed, cried, and learned a bunch. Jim's stories are loving, poignant and interesting. Kelly's are filled with love and humor. I particularly liked the Pizza and Tanqueray story.

- Christina Kyle Casteel
Baton Rouge, LA
Former Aid to US Congressman Richard H. Baker

DEDICATION

To the Ancestors.
All who have gone before, all who will come after...
From you we learn the lessons of life – good, bad, and amusing –
and from them we go forward stronger and wiser than before.

Na zdravi!
Proost!
Skål!
Prost!
Sláinte!
Lechyd da!
Sei gesund!

Cheers to all and good health abounding!

George T. Watters IV
"Big Dad"
Jim's Paternal Grandfather

Other Titles from The Authors

View from the Medicine Lodge

Quiet Autumn Moments

Quiet Winter Moments

The Keepers' Kitchen

Genuine Indian Princess

Keep Calm and Get Social

What Did You Just Say?

Are We Having Fun Yet?

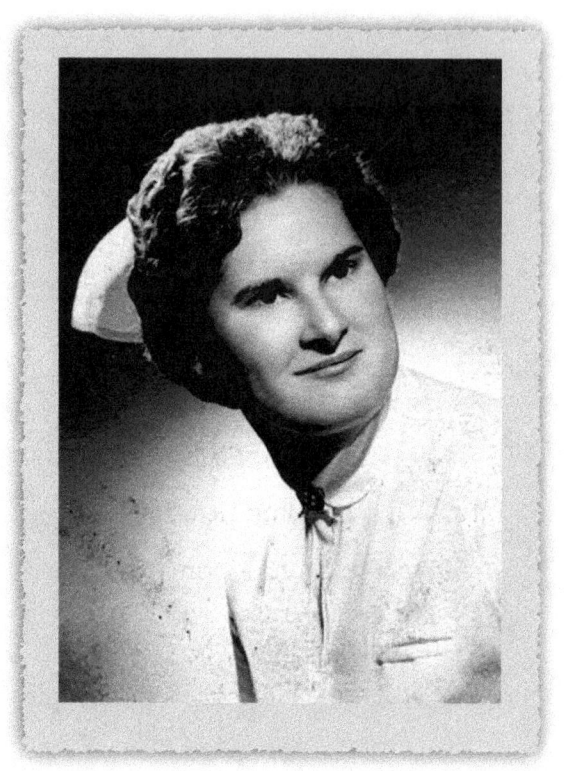

Noreen Sabatka Herron
Kelly's Mom

Table of Contents

Dedication..iii
Other Titles from The Authors v
Table of Contents vii
Preface xi
Introduction xv
Grandma Was a Kitchen Healer 1
Ma Jessie Coffee 5
One Heartbeat Away 9
Grandpa Dug a Well by Hand 13
"The Cat... He Just... Broke!" 19
Bears in the Mulberry Bush 23
Desert Bound 29
Grandpa Was a Dirt Farmer and a Cobbler 33
Mrs. Tinker Taught Me To Trust 39
Grandma Drank Too Much Sake 43
The Vanishing Altar Stone 47
"Remember When...?" 53
The Indian School Incident 55
Indian Time 63
Pies Like Grandma Used To Make 67
Tuesday Nights at Kiddie Park 71
I Love Riding the Rails 75
The Train That Shouldn't Have Become a Ferry 85
The Comet Mound, Place of my Traditions 89
Baba's Great Wisdom 93

Mushroom Double Cheese Pizza & Tanqueray 97
Ladies of Saigon 101
Grandma Violet's Daily Journal 107
Pop Broke his Back 111
Ribbons in the Sky 117
Drew Book, Common Man's Artist 121
Rollercoasters and Death Drops 123
Pop and the Women Elders at the Great House 129
The Only Way out Is Through 135
"See Fred Brown!" 139
They Come in the Wind 143
The Day I Stopped the Pipe 147
Pele Shapes the Sacred Land 151
My First Shoes 155
She Wore Reindeer Antlers & Played a Djembe 159
Hidden Behind the King of Sligo 163
Grandpa Grew Roses 167
Seven Gifts From the Stone of Death 171
Conclusion 201
Cast of Characters, Places and Interesting Things 203
About the Authors 211
More from Jim & Kelly 213
Quiet Moments Series 215
NOTES 219

"See, that's what you outlanders don't understand. Life is for enjoying, not just getting and working, and getting and working."

- Tom Bledsoe, character in The Songcatcher *(2000)*

Nelle Barber Watters
Jim's Mom

Preface

In the spring of 2020 the world changed – drastically. Novel Corona virus (COVID19) was raging through the world and had come to the United States. As Jim was preparing to celebrate his 77th birthday, we at WeWan were preparing to write the third Quiet Moments book for Spring.

One morning, as we were discussing the release date for the book, we sidestepped into the "situation" that had become America. Our governor had just declared a stay-at-home order, "Thirty Days to Stop the Spread" was in full swing, and people were beginning to talk about wearing masks when venturing out into public. Restaurants were closing, grocery shopping became "risky business," and all-but-essential doctor's visits were indefinitely cancelled. No elective surgeries, take out only from restaurants and – strangest of all – a shortage of paper products... namely toilet paper. (huh?!)

The world was coming apart at the seams, it seemed (pardon the pun). We could already see the people around us – friends, family, neighbors – really beginning to stress and become overwhelmed with fear. Suddenly each and every one of our lives was at serious risk. Add to that, COVID19 appeared to be a horrible, lonely, way to die. The fear was well-founded.

From there, our conversation turned to how the Greatest Generation dealt with the crisis of the Great Depression and World War II.

Every one of us has family who lived through that era. They were resourceful, resilient, and refused to be destroyed by the crises all around them. We thought about what we had learned from their Wisdom and began telling each other stories of what we knew of our family's struggles and triumphs.

As it turned out, we talked and told stories for hours! And in so doing, found immense comfort, strength, and inspiration.

"Why not share these stories with the rest of the world?" we asked each other.

And so this book was born.

Together and separately, we began documenting our stories and those of our Elders. What they learned, how they coped, what they taught us. What *we* have learned in our own lives, and how we have improved from those teachings.

Most of all, we laughed. We cried a little, too. Beyond anything else though... we drew together as a team, as a family, and it, overall, gave us the warm fuzzies as we recalled how absolutely *awesome* our Elders were – both in their experiences and in the wisdom they imparted to us.

How fortunate we have been!

And that, Dear Reader, is what we would dearly hope you take from this book. Despite the insanity happening all around us, on so many levels, we are so very fortunate to have life, this life. For, in all its troubles and tribulations, lay hidden like jewels, our great fortunes.

We have air to breathe, roofs over our heads, food on the table, family to love us, friends to tolerate us, each other to laugh and cry with. From the most humble situations to the most affluent, we are blessed with the gift of life, a heart with which to love, and arms with which to hold those we love. (We won't mention the six foot distance concept.)

As humans, we are built to be tribal, clannish, and neighborly. We have weathered countless storms, wars, crises. As Americans, we are strong and proud.

We survive.

As you read this book, we hope you laugh, cry a little, and become inspired – as we did during its inception.

We also hope you begin to know us a little better through meeting our families. Something we bring to you with open hearts and a humility worthy of such amazing human beings.

Everyone has a story... We believe it is our privilege to know of them, and our obligation to keep them alive through the telling. Earnestly, we invite you to follow suit. Tell the stories of your Elders, for they are the well of Wisdom. Tell your own stories... for they are the inspiration and encouragement for the next seven generations to come.

Never let the People die. In our memories and storytelling, they will live forever.

We hope you enjoy this book. We offer it to you from the deepest parts of our souls.

Noreen and baby Kelly

Introduction

Here at the WeWan Institute we believe that, "Everyone has a story, and their story should be heard." In this book, we have collected a few of the stories shared with us... at the knee of our Elders.

We have a philosophy we use to isolate our thinking into a more controlled manner. We envision each person, event or thought living in its own box... on long high shelving, like in Raiders of the Lost Ark!

Each person, each memory, each incident all have their own boxes, and when we open that box, all their connections are there. It never ceases to amaze us how the connections of memories, so intricately intertwined, continually open old connections anew.

With this constant reminder, as we were writing the drafts for each chapter, we were surprised at the amount of other stories we recalled... additional incidents, persons and the time and places involved. As an example, when Jim was writing about his grandfather Jess Barber living on Lower Twin Creek, he remembered two other stories that occurred along that same creek.

At that point we knew this book would be the first in a series of teaching stories from the Circle of Elders in our lives.

It is our hope that as you delve into each chapter, you too will experience this "DNA Déjà vu." If so, write them down to share with family and friends. And if you would like to share them with us, we are always looking for inspirational stories to include in future publications. Just drop us a line at thekeepers@wewan.org with your story.

Each tale in "Grandma was a Kitchen Healer, and Grandpa Grew Roses" contains priceless insight into a world that no longer exists, and yet the wisdom they used to overcome, and achieve, is truly timeless.

Violet Rose Machovec Sabatka
Kitchen Healer

- 1 -
Grandma Was a Kitchen Healer

"Grandma, I have a splinter!"

"Sit down at the kitchen table and I'll get the Nonat."

Oh, the dreaded Nonat, aka "black salve," aka Ichthammol.

Nonat was pronounced "NOH-nahth" except in the Czech language the "n" and "th" are very soft, unlike English. Nevertheless... My grandmother kept it in a drawer under the electric can opener and between the 1970s brown GE refrigerator and gas stove. It smelled like some stinking pit where dinosaurs died eons ago.

Back then it was packaged as a stick. She'd flick on one of the burners of the gas stove and get the end melting. (Sealing wax for the afflicted.) Then on to the painful area it would be spread, bandage applied, and... wait. Wait for several days for it to do its job.

Grandma Violet kept the Nonat for warts, splinters, boils... anything that needed "drawing out," whatever that meant. Always sounded mystical to me. But that "black salve" was one of her secret weapons. It rarely failed to do its magical work. And I always much preferred some stinky black stuff on my finger to the alternative, which was my (RN) mother digging around with a sterilized needle to get at the splinter. Ugh.

The afore mentioned drawer held all manner of magical things. Needles sterilized and set aside solely for poking and prodding (see above), ointments and other smelly stuff, bandages, medical tape, scissors, nail clippers, tweezers, matches. It was like a survival kit from some outdoorsman's satchel.

I can still recall the smell of that drawer as it opened. It meant someone needed patching up.

My Grandma Violet had a flare for "kitchen healing." She'd raised three girls at the back end of the Great Depression, and was the second generation born in America to my mom's family of Bohemian immigrants. Czechoslovakian, that is – not to be confused with the wild and colorful gypsies who were mistakenly associated with that area of Eastern Europe.

My mom and I lived in her parents' humble home in Slavic Village, along with one of my aunts. Dad died before I was born and so mom moved back for emotional support while raising a daughter and having to keep working as an RN. Grandma Violet and Aunt Marlene were surrogate parents to me and I learned a lot from both of them.

Grandma Violet had all manner of tricks up her sleeves for helping us feel better, including the ever present "hanky" tucked into a sleeve cuff – that would be "handkerchief" for the well-to-do folk.

Grandma also always carried candied ginger and mints with her when we traveled – for motion sickness. She seemingly could cure just about any minor ailment from something stashed in a drawer, the pantry, or even the liquor cabinet! There was the dreaded Nonat but there was also Vicks Vapo Rub for my annual winter cold, cough, and sore throat. I was in my twenties before I realized you could wear flannel pajamas without the lingering smell of Vicks on the front of them.

Saltine crackers were not a snack in our household, they were medicine for after you'd puked your guts out and needed a test to see if you could "keep something down." This was no hardship for me. Grandma always had them schmeared with salted butter and blackberry jelly. Yum! And served them with... Vernors. Yuck.

I always hated Vernors. (For those of you not familiar, it is a ginger *soda*.) Growing up in my house, it was used as a curative, not an everyday beverage. To me it always had a much stranger flavor than, say, a Canada Dry type ginger ale – maybe it was the vanilla they add. And for years I associated it with vomit. Not the saltines! Just the Vernors... flat Vernors. Vernors that had deliberately been left exposed to the air to decarbonate and get room temperature. Blek!

I was in my *thirties* before I learned to enjoy it as a tasty beverage. Funny how we associate smells and tastes with emotions. I still have a faded lingering memory every time I pop open a can.

I recall that Grandma used alcohol as medicines more than recreation. Sure, she enjoyed an occasional holiday "highball" but mostly she used distilled spirits as kitchen cures.

There was blackberry brandy for when we had, let's delicately say, "intestinal issues." And Rock n Rye – a tasty concoction of rye whiskey and rock candy, often with an orange slice floating in it. This delectable treat was reserved for when I had a bad cough. It was either given to me straight or in some tea.

I vaguely remember having straight whiskey rubbed on my gums when I was cutting a tooth. It surely did make the pain go away. And grandma gave us Kümmel (a caraway/cumin liqueur) as a digestif when we had bloating and gas. It worked, too!

All these magics I grew up with in an Eastern European home. Grandma taught them to me by example. And, because they were effective, I retained the teachings. I use them to this day.

My Grandma Violet was a kitchen healer.

She used items that we now consider to be "everyday" household objects and substances to comfort and heal the ones she loved. It was the way she learned from her mother, and her mother's mother, etc.

Physicians were very expensive, and employer sponsored health insurance was not widely available before World War II. Blue collar workers, and the European farmers from whom they descended, dealt with minor illness entirely at home.

Herbs, seeds, roots, spices combined with water, fats, or alcohol allowed for a wide range of medicines. Decoctions, ointments/salves/liniments, tinctures, teas. And let's not forget poultices. I've heard so many stories of old European grandmas foisting stinky onion or garlic poultices onto children's chests with *such care and love, doing what they knew from experience would help ease discomfort. There were even herbal bags called **asafetida** that people wore around their necks to ward off all manner of illness. But that's more on the side of my dad's Appalachian family.*

Medicine wo/men and grandmas have been using herbal medicine for eons. They were called healers because, for the most part, the stuff worked! All good outdoorsy folk know that a poison's antidote can be found nearby.

"Modern" medicine has scientifically proven many old timey remedies and we now have them in pill form. Aspirin, digitalis, ephedrine, just to name a few.

Nature has it all laid out for us, grandmas the world over have known it all along.

- 2 -
Ma Jessie Coffee

Ever since the Boston Tea Party when we broke the British tea habit, coffee has been the American brew. The Greatest Generation during the Second World War ran on coffee, black, strong and hot. Back home, most adults and kids in my family drank coffee daily. It was just what we did in rural southern Ohio. In our home, coffee came as beans that we ground in a cast iron meat grinder, and brewed in a percolator. The ever present aroma was as prevalent as fresh baked bread. Coffee was a staple and life was simple and good.

Coffee was served in many forms. If we had been good kids, mom would make us Coffee Toast, a delectable treat of toasted homemade bread, buttered with sugar sprinkled on top... and hot coffee drizzled on it! What's not to like about that... butter, sugar, toast and hot coffee! We preferred this over "store bought" donuts or pastries.

Our coffee habit began in the morning with the first pot brewing before sunrise – always on the flat-top cast iron coal stove. We never had soda pop in our home and this was in the days before Kool-Aid. We had two choices, well water or coffee. We drank a lot of coffee.

My dad's mom was known affectionately, by family and friends alike, as Ma Jessie. In the restaurant at Jimmie's Place she would offer up an extraordinary southern hospitality treat, Ma Jessie Coffee. With her combination of loving mama, barista... and magician... she would enchant one and all with this most delectable cup of indulgence. Pouring a half cup of steaming hot strong brew into a mug, she would top it off with an equal amount of rich country cream and a heaping tablespoon of sugar. Oh my, it was "hot liquid candy!"

"Ma Jessie"
Jessie Ada Lucretia Price Watters

It is said that in France they have perfected the brewing of coffee. With their distinctive names I suppose the French would need to create a new title similar to their *le café normal,* le café americain, etc. In Appalachia, we're not so "hoity toity" as to call it, "le café jessie." We simply call this southern lady-like coffee, Ma Jessie Coffee. Even if nameless, it would still be a cup of "hot liquid candy!"

During my tour in the Navy, a pot of "joe" was ever present – black, hot and strong. I was so grateful for the privilege of a cuppa to kept me alert and focused.

Throughout the next half century hot java was, and still is, a staple that I truly enjoy. Included below is my homage to my lifelong affair with the "magic roasted bean." My ever present companion now, for seven decades.

How easy it is to, as the saying goes, refill the pot with the joy of just a few pleasant memories. Why not take a moment now and ponder on a time when your life was filled with similar pleasantries. These are times of stress that demand our attention... but a bit of daydreaming of yesteryear may just be what the doctor ordered, to rejuvenate and restore an otherwise downer day. Try it!

Now I gotta go, my cup's full of steaming joe, and I'm ready for the day!

Java, the Path Is Long

Excerpted from: **View From The Medicine Lodge**

Drip... drip... drip...
trickle... flow...
gush in steam,
vapors of mountains and streams,
in jungle green, in rich verdant.

Long journey from hand picked,
to burlap on backs.
Spread and sorted,
grade dependent on color and nose...
again in burlap, or paper.

Trucks... crate and box...
ship dark and stifle...
bobbing on waves of green,
docked at last, a port strange to the homeland.

Trucks once more.
To shop and store.
Ground at last in cup or glass,
our nirvana achieved.
A cup of java, essence of our breeze.

Ah, coffee... the "joy of the brew!"

Cliff Herron
Wedding Day, March 20, 1965
Brooklyn Heights, Ohio

- 3 -
ONE HEARTBEAT AWAY

I'm quite certain she knew there would eventually be heartache in the decision to marry a man 20 years her senior. But the love was deep... strong... undeniable.

He was so handsome, so very full of life. One of those men who everyone wanted to be near – men and women, children and adults, all. Charismatic, kind, quick to laugh and have fun, slow to anger. Born and raised in the rural, mountain, coal-mining towns of Appalachia, he had moved to the big city in search of a better life for his family. Now he had two adult girls who adored him and a marriage whose life was at its end. These things happen, sadly. With the end of one thing, however, it makes room for the beginning of another.

She was young and inexperienced, a nursing student, with dreams and all the excitement of a life just beginning. Raised in a community of "old country" values and work ethics, she still lived with her parents. That is what was expected of an unmarried girl in those days. Dad wanted (expected) her to marry a doctor. She just wanted to finish her education and discover what awaited her as a career nurse.

Destiny... fate... luck... Whatever you choose to call it, it has its own ideas of how life will play out for each of us. I am convinced it is a good thing we don't know what is to happen in the next day, week, or year. Sometimes it would be unbearable, I suspect.

How do you know love when it happens to you? Most of us can't really answer that... We just know.

And she did. She knew this love was "it" when it happened to her. It was an unpopular choice in the eyes of many around her, including her father. The age difference, the cultural difference... a divorced man! Quite a shock, but this love was not to be denied.

They were married on the first day of spring, it was a new beginning for him and the start of a life she'd never even dreamed of. By that time, everyone had come to understand why this man was so special. One couldn't help but love him.

By Thanksgiving she was pregnant. So much excitement. They talked, and planned, and picked out names. You see... he wanted this child so very much. Although he'd lost two boys when they were babies, and he'd raised two daughters already, he wanted a little girl who looked just like his lovely new bride. He enjoyed being a parent and couldn't wait to share his life and affection with a new child.

The holidays came and went, a whirlwind of family and celebrating. The new year began and they settled in to await the summer arrival of their precious gift.

January 4. It changed everything. A day that would haunt her heart for the rest of her life.

In their modest little apartment, on the near west side of Cleveland, she awoke that morning, as usual, lying next to the love of her life, ready to begin a new day. But he... they... never did again.

It was over before it had even begun, really.

He was dead at 45, she was widowed at 25. Suddenly alone and lost and scared. Dreams shattered. A baby growing inside her who would now never know his love.

Can you even begin to comprehend such a scene? The devastation. The finality. The horror.

The plans. The dreams. The hope. Gone. All of it gone.

Can you imagine?

I can... I was there that day. Well, maybe not how you might think.

January 4, 1966 changed my life also. I was there the day my mother lost the love of her life.

He was my dad – and he left before I ever really got here.

I would never know him, never hear his voice, never feel his arms around me. Would not learn to fish and hunt – or how to find wild plants in the eastern woodlands. It would take me almost 30 years to re-connect with his family, and my sisters, and begin to understand the man he'd been.

And so that is how my life started... Not yet born, and already I'd experienced a devastating loss that would impact every day of the rest of my life.

And I wish I could tell you that was the only loss I knew. But unfortunately loss is something I've come to know all too well in my five plus decades.

But that is not the message I want you to take from this narrative. No.

I've had an extraordinary life so far. It has not been very conventional by any means, but it has been memorable.

It took me a long time to realize abandonment wasn't around every corner. Or, perhaps I should say, to accept the idea. I still struggle with a very deep fear of loss.

But with every negative there is a positive. And it has taught me to live with no regrets. And that, in turn, has allowed me to know the value of every relationship and all the emotion that accompanies them. Love, laughter, angst, disappointment, excitement, hope... all of it.

Leave no words unspoken, my friend. Do not assume you – nor anyone around you – is guaranteed tomorrow, or even the next moment. Life moves fast, and it changes in a heartbeat. Literally. We are all one heartbeat away from goodbye.

Live with no regrets. Say yes to the experiences that call to you. Say yes to the people who excite you. Say yes to your dreams. And live with complete awareness and gratitude. This is a precious gift you've been given. Live. It. Fully.

Old Hand Dug Well
with Well House

- 4 -
Grandpa Dug a Well by Hand

In other chapters of this book I write about my grandfather Jess Barber, because he was pivotal in my life and was a very unique human being. Every story I tell about him reflects how he imprinted me in my youth and made me a better person.

In my early formative years I lived in a small town on the Ohio River called Buena Vista, and my grandparents lived just a "good stretch of the legs" up Lower Twin Creek holler. I enjoyed the walk and made it as often as I could, because it was the journey... not the destination!

The journey was pretty much always the same... and yet always unique.

Have you ever experienced walking barefoot on a one hundred year old sidewalk of well worn sandstone? Even on the hottest days of summer the huge slabs of ancient grayed stone were always cool to the touch. Walking the short distance to the highway, I often let my mind wander, thinking about the feet of the people who had walked on those same stones since the 1850's. I passed Mr. Francis' weathered Victorian two-story home and side yard garden with its tempting ripe tomatoes in season, stopping at the water pump in front of the school for a big drink of its icy well water.

Crossing US Route 52 was dangerous because the traffic never slowed down. It was the equivalent of an interstate back then and, because of its importance, it was a well traveled highway. "Look both ways, stop look both ways again, and then once more..." was the drill when crossing.

As I would pass Mr. Miller's General Store I would always wave and say hello to the men setting on the front porch. Being respectful was expected of youngsters in our village, and the old men would often reciprocate with a piece of stick candy in return. I always enjoyed that part of it.

Beyond the highway I turned uphill onto the old Tram Road along the side of the creek gurgling below. The soft silt dust that covered the road would squeeze between my bare toes and felt swell... and it tickled, too!

Around the bend, there was the shale bank that had turned to clay below. On days when we children gathered there to swim, we would fetch a pail of creek water, climb back up to the roadway and dump it on the clay. This made a slick slide back down to the swimming hole below. I recall the boisterous taunts of the boys, and the squeals of delight as the girls also took turns sliding down the slick wet clay into the swimming hole.

Beyond the swimming place, the road became a "tree tunnel," covered by the branches of century-plus old sycamores, oaks and hickory trees that lined the way. Such things are what bring back pleasant memories and create dreams for those who have never experienced such pleasure.

A little further up the road was the swinging bridge that crossed over to the other bank. It was exciting each time I would cross the bridge high above the water.

Suspended by two rusty cables, and two more for hand rails, the wooden deck always swayed back-and-forth with each step. In the spring there was usually a good amount of water running, but by late summer it dried to almost a trickle. Most of us thought it was a wonderful experience, but some believed that the old cables would snap at any moment... "plunging them to their death" in the ravine below. It wasn't very high, only an eight or ten or foot drop. To the best of my knowledge those old cables never broke, but some of the floorboards would rot away and then be replaced.... like everything around, it was really old, and it had history.

I followed the well worn footpath that went between the corn field to the right and the ancient barbed wire and black locust post fence. At the peak of summer it seemed as if you were walking in another tree tunnel, the corn growing seven or eight feet tall on one side and the trees and brush equally on the other.

It was magical.

The footpath ended on the dusty graveled Lower Twin Creek Road. Heading up the hill towards my grandpa's home, I would often stop at the well alongside the road, dipping the ladle into the bucket of water on the wooden wellhouse, refreshing myself with the sweetwater.

Crossing the old wooden bridge over the trickle of a little unnamed creek, I could see my grandparents home.

I told you... it was always a journey, a kid's adventure! When you're young, everything should be an adventure.

Their cottage was humble, built somewhere in the mid 1800s. It was a single-story Cape Cod, a sloping front yard before it, and had a porch running the full front length. It was comfortable and small, no more than 500 sqft. Through the front door, there was a bedroom to the left and the living room to the right. On the back wall of the living room was the staircase leading up to the attic with another bedroom. The door beneath the stairs went to the kitchen and storage room. In the distant past someone had constructed a lean-to which served as their summer kitchen.

The place was heated with a warm morning stove – the kitchen coal stove was only for cooking.

Under most standards it would be considered a primitive home. With an old barn at the roadside and the outhouse down the path that went along the edge of the long, bottomland field.

The journey to my grandfather's house was always an adventure, but what happened next was an education that imprinted me with knowledge that can only be acquired by apprenticing with a man of extraordinary skills. My grandfather was many things, but what he did best of all was to teach by example.

I suppose some modern folk would call a well drilling company to come out and punch a hole in the ground, put a hand pump on the top of the pipe and say here it is. That would not work for my grandfather Jess. He was just too old fashioned. Too stubborn.

This well had to be dug by hand.

It had all started when I was sitting by my grandfather at church. In the middle of a song, possibly "Onward Christian Soldiers," he leaned over and whispered in my ear.

"Grandson, could you please help me with a chore? I need to dig a new well."

"Yes'siree Bob," I whispered. How exciting! I'd never seen a well dug by hand, and I loved hard work. (Still do!)

Early the following Saturday, I joined my grandpa behind his house, where he had, using his mule and rock sled, fetched a good pile of flat stones from the creek in a variety of shapes and sizes. From these, he hand selected shapes, each for a specific purpose.

He had already begun the work by the time I arrived. The hole was about five or six feet deep, and was masterfully lined with the stones, interlocking them together, they pressed towards the outside into the soft clay soil of the wall. How they stayed there, defying gravity, had to be magic.

The work was pretty straightforward. Grandpa would dig at the bottom, and fill a bucket with the dirt. Then I pulled it up with the rope and dumped it on a pile a few steps away. Even the pile of dirt was strategically placed so that runoff water would not flood into the well itself. Bucket after bucket we continued to dig the well. Around fifteen to twenty feet deep, grandpa told me, we should hit a known aquifer of sweet water that was filtered through the ancient glacier moraine gravels. It was nature's way of providing pure safe drinking water.

Bucket by bucket, stone by stone. It was the rhythm that day, filled with random chatter, as he taught me how he was placing the stones, and shared stories of his childhood. With each bucket the well went deeper, the pile of dirt higher and the stone piles disappeared into the hole.

At last my grandfather said, "There it is, we have water, Jimmie!"

He sent up a few more buckets of mud and clay, and then he asked to have some flat stones from the last pile, to line the bottom. I could hear him sloshing about in the bottom of the well and at last he hollered up, "Jimmie, tie that rope off good to the apple tree over by the shed." I did as he asked, tying it off with a bowline knot that my dad had taught me. I pulled on it real hard and shouted down the hole, "It's tied off good, grandpa!"

It wasn't but a minute until I saw his head come above ground as he pulled himself out of the hole to sit on the edge, looking back down and said, "Praise the Lord, I think we got a good well!"

We placed an old door over the opening for safety, and cleaned up in a wash pan. We sat down in the shade of the house on an old handmade wooden bench, leaning back against the wall. To celebrate the accomplishment, we chatted about the experience while enjoying a strong cuppa Folgers "Mountain Grown" coffee.

The last job to be done was completed the next day. Grandpa had assembled some flat, milled boards he had sawn, and in short order we had built a well house to cover the hole. It was a box with a hinged wood lid to keep critters out, and sheltered by a double shed roof perched on four by fours. We shingled the roof with hand froe'd cedar splits. The now spotless galvanized bucket that we had used to haul out the dirt, and the stones into the well, was now the well bucket… with rope attached.

The first time we dropped the bucket down into the hole you could hear a great splash at the bottom. The water had risen several feet into the stone lined shaft, ensuring a good supply of drinking water. Grandpa pulled up a good half bucket of the first water from his new well. Tipping it to his mouth as if it were a coffee cup, he took a long sweet swig! Then held the bucket for me while I did the same. Ma Gertie had come out to celebrate, with a drinking dipper in her hand. Ever so daintily she dipped into the bucket and took a sip of the same water.

The Barbers had a new sweetwater well, one of the best I've ever seen! I was so proud of my grandfather and his pioneer skill sets… and he didn't have some stranger drill into his sacred land!

Today pioneering skills, such as digging a well by hand, are a lost art. We find that it is much easier to use modern conveniences like well-drilling machines to replace the hard work needed to accomplish such tasks. It is common to buy a new tool to replace one that was damaged, or hire someone to do work around the house. That is good, but is it possible that by doing so we have contributed to those "Lost Arts?"

The next time you break a handle on a shovel, rather than buying a new shovel, buy a new handle instead, and replace the broken one yourself. The few minutes involved in this simple act will help connect you to your past generations. The "feel good factor" of accomplishing a lost art task will not add to your resume, but will add to your ancient pioneer skills.

Life isn't about how much we can accumulate or buy, but is about learning and perfecting those skills that connect us to the past seven generations, and the next seven generations not yet born.

- 5 -
"The Cat... He Just... Broke!"

It was the summer of 1984 and I was with my dear high school friend Rolf and his mom Inga Maj in the little Swedish town of Dals-Ed. He had been an exchange student at Hawken School in Gates Mills, Ohio and we met in 1981 when I was a sophomore. He went back to Sweden the following year but we kept in touch, always planning to see one another again.

Now I'd graduated, and we were spending the summer together. After some weeks spent in St. Pete, Florida (my family's summer hangout place), we'd left the US and traveled back to the little town where he lived with his mom. It was the first time I'd ever been out of the country and so many things were new for me, "the city girl," especially the rural setting of this beautiful place.

Rolf's uncle Brör had a summer cabin out in the middle of nowhere – *ingenstans*, they might say. Uncle Brör's cabin was the most picturesque thing I'd ever seen in my scant eighteen years. And it remains in a secret little corner of my heart, a place where time stood still and postcards could actually exist.

It was deep in the pine forest, which are abundant in that part of the world. A dark blue lake nearby for fishing, and a fire ring outside for socializing and wood fire cooking. There was no running water, no electricity. An outhouse, complete with the crescent moon cutout, stood out back, well away from the cabin. It was something I'd never seen before and didn't really believe still existed anywhere.

In Sweden, in the height of summer, though the sun sets after 10pm and rises again before 4am, there is a light that always remains in the sky. But even the woods darken during the summer months. And in this quaint little cabin, I clearly remember lighting candles on the kitchen table as the conversation went long into the evening.

On one of those long summer days, in that long ago time, we were invited to dinner at the cabin, including some friends of Inga Maj's who were visiting from Germany. Rolf and I took a separate car, enjoying a leisurely summer drive through the countryside.

As a side note...This was the summer I learned that road trips to seemingly nowhere would be one of my great loves of life. There was always a treasure to be found along the way – a lake, an old bridge, a moose crossing the road! This remains a favorite past time of mine even today. Rolf taught me well. But that is a story for a later time.

The plan that summer day was that Inga Maj would join us later and she would be bringing the cat, Pissen. Rolf and I arrived hours before Inga Maj did. We spent time visiting, walking through the woods, exploring down to the lake. It was the height of summer and yet cool enough for a jacket in the evening. The tall and fragrant pine trees were everywhere, the lake water was crystal clear, and the smell of a wood cooking fire lured us back to the cabin.

Just as the fire was really getting going, Inga Maj's Saab came into the "driveway." We heard the parking gear engage, and we all watched as she jumped swiftly from the car, looking distressed. She was a bit out of breath, and was making noises like something very bad – very bad indeed – had happened.

I remember sitting there on the log and becoming alarmed, it looked like she was bringing bad news. I was immediately concerned that she was alright, yet she looked just fine!

She came around the back of her little car and opened the rear passenger door. The cat jumped out, and promptly ran like hellfire. And Inga Maj blustered to all of us, in her British-influenced Swedish accent, "The cat... He... He just... he just... brrrooohhhke!"

Well! That *was* alarming!

My eighteen year old mind was grinding, trying to comprehend what a broken cat actually means to a native Swedish speaker speaking British English when she's upset. Whatever it was, she was very fraught and was finding it difficult to calm down, despite the fact that the cat had jumped out of the car and run off looking perfectly healthy, albeit frazzled, but most importantly, in one piece!

Apparently I wasn't the only one who was not understanding her. Rolf looked equally confused and the poor German folk... they were quite lost if the looks on their faces were anything to judge.

So Inga Maj did as she always did when she wasn't readily getting her point across: she began gesturing wildly with her hands and arms, and raising the volume of her words.

"We were driving – I was driving – here, and all of a sudden, he just brrrrroke! Halfway here. All over the back seat of the car! I don't know why. He just brrrrroke!" And she began gesturing

Rolf Andersson with Pissen Katten
at Uncle Brör's Lake Cabin
Dalsland, Sweden

with her hands, illustrating something flying from her mouth and onto the ground.

Aha.... now we were getting somewhere! The cat was still in one piece and fine. He had vomited. Puked. Did the rainbow yawn. Tossed his cookies. You get the picture. This was a much less alarming conclusion than what I had originally been imagining.

Rolf jumped up to help her, they got things cleaned up, Pissen eventually came back to join us. It was a lovely rest of the evening. We all enjoyed a delicious dinner of moose steak, cooked over an open fire. We talked late into the night, then drove home through the forest to the little town of Ed.

But I never forgot that scene and being told the cat had just broke!

I was really frightened and alarmed in those initial moments. In this instance, it was a case of language barrier, but it shows my point.

Fear is an illusion.

It's nothing more than an emotional reaction to unfamiliar events or circumstances, over which you feel you have no control, and therefore are vulnerable in some way. Oftentimes, the things that scare you at the moment are, in hindsight, not nearly as bad as you originally think.

In my story above, I really thought something had gone terribly wrong and that maybe someone had been hurt. As we learned more about the circumstances, we were assured that everything would be just fine. My fear was an illusion of my own making.

Watching someone else being upset or distressed is alarming. We want to help and make things better, fix things. It's a natural and wonderful part of being human.

Next time you find yourself afraid, remember to pull back the curtain of fear's illusion, educate yourself on the facts, and take control of yourself and whatever part of the situation you can.

The cat may be broke, but you don't have to be.

- 6 -
Bears in the Mulberry Bush

When I was a youngster I loved to hunt and fish… alone. This may sound unusual to most but it was just the way I was. My dad was not so fond of it, and I guess my mom either, but they always supported my choice. Oftentimes I would go up onto the mountain above the house in the little village where we lived. There I would make my camp in the usual spot along the edge of the sandstone cliffs. My folks could see the light of my campfire, and the smoke signals that I would send out each morning and evening, to let my mom know I was OK.

This was in the time when children were allowed the freedom to explore, by themselves, the area around them. We were countryfolk, and kids grew up much sooner than they do today. I can't speak for my siblings, for we have never really had a conversation about this, but as for me… I enjoyed that freedom. I know that my mom must have been panic stricken at times, for just a couple or three years earlier I'd been hit by a car and was not always in the best of health.

It was such a great experience on the ledge at the mouth of a small cave, where generations of my Panji Seepe/Shawnee ancestors had made their camp for a lookout up and down the broad Buena Vista reach of the Ohio River. It was a wide, safe outcropping and the cave was deep enough to protect me from any sudden rain storms. It had been a well used shelter for a very long time. The ceiling and front walls were coated with the soot from the countless fires built deep in the cave. Scratched into this coating were images of past hunts and the name-marks of those who used this place long ago. It was as if the walls were talking to me… and I listened. The perfect place for a youngster to discover his powers.

It was on one of those camp-outs that I had the encounter with the Bears. I'd been fishing in a pond perhaps half a mile north of my camp cave. The pond had been created by rainwater and small creeks pouring into the cavity where the Buena Vista Sandstone Company quarried building block material in the 1800's. It was a cool little body of water, maybe twenty by fifty feet and no more than five to seven feet deep at best. I'd done well and had several bluegill and a couple of big crappie in my burlap game bag. They added to the rabbit I taken with my bow and arrow... we would eat well at home.

Growing up country, it wasn't so much that I hunted and fished, but that I had learned how to provide for our family. We had hams and bacon hanging, canned meats and of course my dad would bring home fresh meat from the butcher every weekend.

Thinking back, a skillet of bluegill and crappie fillets, double dipped in seasoned corn meal and flour, fried in lard, was surely a treat. It was full on summer and we had fresh string beans, dug potatoes and sweet corn along with just-ripened watermelon. Concorde grapes, big as golf balls and giant purple plums were coming on also. In the summer we feasted on what we had grown and harvested. Compared with folks in the city, we may have been"dirt poor," but we were well fed.

I'd been heading back towards the trail down to town, whistling whatever tunes came to my head, oblivious to my surroundings. This was not how I usually acted in the woods, for there were always timber rattlers and copperhead snakes in abundance, soaking in the sun on the trails, but it was a beautiful day and well... my guard was down.

As I crested a small ridge and started to drop down into a swale left by the stone cutters a good century before, I followed the deer trail towards the south. Stopping in a small clumping where mulberry trees were growing, it was my intent to harvest a few handfulls to take home. I loved mulberries as well as everyone else in my family.

Reaching into one of the larger bushes I was busy stuffing hands full of berries into my bag. Some would say having fresh caught fish in the same container with mulberries might just taint the flavor. I would assume that those same folks didn't know how to wash food when they brought it in to the kitchen. They'd all be fine when I got home.

As I was putting the last of the berries in my poke, I heard a bit of rustling in the low bushes behind me and I turned to see a little face stick out from beneath the greenery... and then another, and yet another... Three little bear cubs!

A split second later my mind and demeanor shifted. I was old enough to know that if there were cubs in the bushes, mama would not be far away.

As I gingerly stepped out of the tree stand onto the trail towards the river, all hell broke loose! The bushes beyond the cubs exploded with one very angry and very protective mama sow. I smelled her breath as she growled.

My feet were already moving away!

Now most countryfolk know that you just can't out run a bear. I was quite aware of that fact. So as I was moving as fast as my little legs could carry me, I had the good sense to throw my poke with the fish and berries – and the fat rabbit – back towards the cubs. Not missing a step and not slowing down.

In all the action, I also dropped my handmade bow and arrows along the path. I wasn't about to come back to pick them up right now, as there were more pressing issues... behind me!

I could feel the pads of her big feet clawing at the dirt behind me as she was either charging, or "bluff charging." At that moment I didn't know whether this would be my day of reckoning or reprieve, because it sounded like she was gaining on me quickly!

Whether it was good sense, good luck, or the good Lord just protecting this kid, as I came to the top of the grade towards the river, I glanced over my shoulder and mama bear had started to head back to her cubs.

As I crossed Highway 52, and walked towards our house down the newly oiled gravel lane known as Main Street, I was still shaking inside. I smelled of sweat and dust, and that acidic smell that comes from adrenaline pumping. I don't suppose many people outside Appalachia can even identify that elusive smell, one that predator animals are keen on. It doesn't matter whether you're fearful or not, it happens during that fight or flight instant.

I stopped at the two room school house pump, to compose and wash myself up a bit. I had promised mom that I would bring some fish home, but now I not only didn't have fish, or that big rabbit, or that small passel of sweet mulberries... but even the burlap poke that she had given me to carry the meat home in was back on that path with the bears.

I was coming home empty-handed... not how I expected the day to end.

As I entered the back door making sure to clean my boots first, mama said, "Son, what happened?" Moms have that special sense to know when something bad has happened, or when you've done something bad... and they instinctively know the difference.

Mama dipped us both a glass of cool water from the galvanized bucket in the summer kitchen, and we went back outside and sat on the stoop. I told her what had happened and apologized for not bringing the meat home that day. I felt real bad. A lot more bad than any fear instilled in me. I had learned a great lesson through this experience, that you never lose your focus, and be aware at all times of what is around you.

That hyper-vigilance certainly kept me safe during my war years.

She wasn't angry, nor overly protective, she just put her arm around my shoulder and said, "I'm glad you're OK, boy."

The next morning I retraced my steps up the mountain and down into the swale where the bears had been eating mulberries. I had a handful of fair size rocks that I flung hard into the bushes, to spook out anything that may be hiding within them. I pelted the shrubs hard. Not a sound, not a movement. Nothing. For good measure I hurled the area with a couple more good sized rocks. Nothing. Safe. They'd gone.

About halfway down the trail, I found my bow and arrows, untouched. I picked them up and put them over my shoulder, and moved on.

A few steps beyond the berry patch on the trace heading north I spotted the burlap poke. Retrieving it I saw that it had been ripped apart on one side. All that was left inside were a few fish scales and some berry stains. The string that held the rabbit to my poke had ripped away... along with my big fat rabbit!

They had made a feast out of my fishing and hunting endeavors.

That day I returned to the pond and pulled out five big crappie, and two bluegill. Didn't see any sign of rabbit or squirrel, so I returned home that afternoon with the fish strung on my bow string, and one ripped up bag.

Sitting on the stoop after dinner, I darned up the tear in my burlap bag, making it as good as new.

Misadventures like this have foddered many engaged audiences for decades. This is a true story, no exaggeration, just fact. I lived in a different time, and in the Appalachian foothills... a different world than most.

I am blessed that I had the opportunity to live in the shadows of those wonderful mountains and hills, and on the mud flats of the river that my ancestors called the Spaylaywitheepi... the mighty waterway that opened to the world beyond the ancient Appalachian Mountains. It was the mystical place of my youth, where I learned my magic, and became a strong two-legged.

It's not that my life was more special than anyone else's. Everyone has memories that make them the "Who that they are." I am not unique, I just came from a different time and place.

Do you recall stories, told by your grandparents and elders, that intrigued you... entranced you? If so, honor them and write them down for the generations to come to enjoy and learn. The stories that your family shared with you are your history and tell of how you became.

Everyone has a story! What is yours?

Some Bear Facts:

The black bear is between four to seven feet in length, and two to three feet tall. Its small eyes, rounded ears and long snout, along with its large shaggy haired body, fits our concept of the "perfect" bear. It is rarely dangerous to humans, unless threatened.

Bears have always been native to Ohio and were said to have been in great numbers at the turn of the nineteenth century. The Ursus Americanus, American black bear, were nearly driven to extinction by early settlers' hunting. Today the settlers are gone, and woodlands have regrown, and the bears are returning from neighboring states to establish home ranges of their own.

The Ohio Division of Wildlife has an acronym for their rules on what to do when faced with a black bear. It's called AWARE.

- *Act calm and do not run.*
- *Warn the bear that you are near – talk in a firm, calm voice.*
- *Allow space between you and the bear. Step aside and back slowly away. Do not make the bear feel trapped or threatened.*
- *Raise your hands above your head to appear larger if the bear approaches. Clap your hands or shout to scare the bear away.*
- *Exit the area – which, to most folks, seems to be the most practical advice of all.*

- 7 -
Desert Bound

Bryan and I fell in love with the desert in 1990. The Sonoran desert, that is – greater Phoenix area – where the sky seems eternally blue, the sunsets more spectacular than imagination could create, the plants/trees look like something out of the Flintstones, and the summer temperatures soar while the humidity plummets.

It was so very different than our Ohio home climate – we loved the abundant sun and the warm temperatures. Neither one of us was ever a fan of the cold dark Ohio winters. We longed to make a life in the beautiful sun-drenched desert but, for decades, couldn't see a way to do it. Family, work, business, etc.

We contented ourselves with summer vacations to the area over twenty five years and continued to long for a home there.

Fast forward to the late fall of 2016. Have you ever heard the phrase, "All the cards fell into place?" Yes, that is what happened.

Suddenly it was the right moment for Bryan to begin a job search in Phoenix. Suffice to say, the stars aligned and our decades long wait was about to be over. Both Jim and I began packing for the move as the decision was made to move both business partners' households at the same time.

And pack we did. Jim was an expert at cross-country moves, I was not. I'd moved exactly three times in my fifty years. And *none* of them were farther than 20 miles. Bryan and I had built that house in 1992 and had lived there ever since – the idea of emptying it was beyond daunting. It was far easier for me to go down to southern Ohio and help Jim pack than it was for me to pack my own things.

Oh, the sheer *volume* we'd accumulated in a quarter century! It felt at times insurmountable. I'd actually been dreading it since the moment I knew it really had to be done. No more dreaming about the move, it was actually happening. And the renovations required simply could not happen with the amount of "stuff" in the house. Not to mention that our realtor wanted it empty when it went on the market.

Bryan accepted a position in May, and we wanted the house on the market by August. Three months to pack, renovate, and get out. Yikes!

The dread turned into near panic as we got farther into the process. I realized that I'd kept things because I was afraid if I let them go it would mean letting go of my memories of the person who was no longer in my life.

I connected memories with physical items.

If I let the physical item go, was I allowing the respect, and memories, and love to go too? Did it mean I simply didn't care anymore? That it wasn't important to me any longer? Was I disrespecting the dead and lost?

I'd had this view of keeping memories in physical things for decades. (I've lost many loved ones in my life, unfortunately.) Therefore, I had many items stashed away which I hadn't had contact with since the loss. Couldn't get rid of them, but couldn't face them either.

When it was time to empty the house, *all* those holders of memories had to be addressed once and for all, lest we drag many pounds of unwanted items across the country only to clutter up a new home. And besides, we'd have to pay to move every single pound of those, as well as keep them in storage until we found a permanent home in Phoenix. Not happening.

This was really overwhelming for me. Many days spent encountering stashed stuff that I hadn't seen in years. It was emotionally exhausting as it caused me to have to face and work through several sad memories a day.

Jim stayed beside me and was there to comfort me when I cried and to talk me through why it was ok to get rid of things, and which things would be let go.

As I got into it further, I realized that the things I'd pitched or donated days before hadn't wiped out my memories as I had feared. All the emotions were still there, with or without the item in my possession. This was indeed a revelation to me!

I got bolder as that summer progressed. The more I kept inside by letting go of the outside, the stronger and more free I felt. It was amazingly cathartic and became less of an emotional drain every week.

By the end of the summer, I'd allowed myself two small boxes which I labeled, "Kelly's Sentimentals." I put in them the things I truly was not able to part with at that time. And believe me when I tell you that two small boxes was huge progress!

Those boxes came with me to Arizona. I eventually made two for Bryan also. Everything else was donated, sold, or went out in the garbage. I've since become a real stickler for not over-saving sentimental items. It's not that I've grown the least bit cold or indifferent. I've simply learned that it's ok to let go of the physical.

Things don't hold memories... your brain and your heart hold the memories.

While it is wonderful to save and use things from those we love, those who were near and dear to us, not everything is useful to keep. Sometimes our desire to hold onto someone we've lost – either through death or heartbreak – can overwhelm the practicality of moving on with our life.

Recognize that your love is not tied to an object. Love, memories, respect – all those wonderful emotions that come from allowing someone to be an important piece of your life – will stay with you forever and ever. The object you grasp onto is a mere shadow of what lies in your heart.

Let go of the idea that love and memories can be lost. Your lost loved ones don't live in things. They live in **you**!

Trust yourself to hold onto what is special in a way that requires nothing but your heart and mind.

Grandpa Jess Barber

- 8 -
Grandpa Was a Dirt Farmer and a Cobbler

Grandpa Jess enjoyed touching the earth, checking its moisture and mix by compressing it between his hands, sifting it through his fingers and even tasting it for salts and sweets – all information that helps the farmer. It seemed that he was always doing something that connected to the soil.

Be it hand-digging a well, raking leaves for compost or, as I would like to brag about my grandpa, being a dirt farmer. Home garden farmers still need cash. Without a cash crop, most need a "day job."

At the age of sixteen he was working in one of the several shoe factories in Portsmouth, Ohio. Like many of his generation, his life was full. As a child he lived with his family as tenant farmers near Rush, Ohio. He loved being on the "farm" and doing the necessary chores. Sometime in his early teens his family moved from his beloved farm to town.

His connection with the earth was never interrupted, though. Before going to work in the morning he would tend to the garden alongside the boarding house in North Portsmouth, where his family lived. Finishing his work at the factory, he would return to his weeding, planting and harvesting. His connection with the earth was biblical. He believed that, "from dust he came and to dust he will return." He never lost his connection with the earth.

By the age of twenty six, he had been married for three years and was now working as a "laster" at the Selby shoe factory. He and his bride, Gertie, lived in a rented room in the back of a house in town. And yes, they had a garden.

Throughout his life he lived in several different places, but he never moved from the county in which he had been born – Scioto

County, Ohio. He did travel to Virginia, Florida and elsewhere to visit with his children, but always came home where his roots were the deepest.

I don't recall anyone ever telling me about when my grandparents moved to the westernmost part of the county. This added another hour and a half of drive time each day, but he was back living on the "land." The daily drive from the shoe factory took him 24 miles west on US 52 with a short jaunt up Lower Twin Creek Road.

He spoke often about his early life in the small village of Rush, on the west side of the Scioto River, his resting place today. Of the several places he had lived, his home on Lower Twin Creek was the one place he held most dear. I know this because he told me so!

I recalled him first living in a small home at the bend of Twin Creek Street in the village of Buena Vista. From our front yard I could see his front porch, just a couple hundred feet away. This allowed me to just walk down the lane to spend special hours with my beloved grandpa. I was blessed.

This changed when he moved less than a mile away, up the gravel road on Lower Twin.

It might as well have been a journey of one hundred years in the past, for that's when his second home up the holler had been built. In truth, with the exception a couple of old trailers, the homes, fields, foot paths down to the creek, and even the old wooden bridges spanning the many small seeded streams, were of that era. He would share that, "This is like being back with Ma and Pa up in Rush." He had come home.

The old cottage and outbuildings were all close to the road, and there was about a 300 foot reach of bottom land behind the cottage. That was the field he farmed every year.

My first remembrance was of him working the ground guiding an ancient plow behind a brown and black draft mule whose sire was of Belgian stock. Mules in general are large animals and this animal, "Jack," was a hinny, a male about as tall as any I've ever seen... Not counting his long ears.

The plow itself was a well worn "lightweight" No.100 Bucher Gibbs, mould-board with a colter blade that broke the ground before the blade itself. It cut and rolled open clean furrows to about six inches deep and ten wide. The whole rig weighed near seventy pounds. Keeping this farm implement upright and in a straight line, with only the two wooden handles attached to the frame, had to have been an extraordinary challenge.

Ol' Jack was hitched up to a single tree with the plow-rig attached behind. Grandpa always worked the field shirtless. In my mind's eye, I picture a middle aged man, dark brown neck and arms with a much lighter white wiry muscular frame, and the traces draped over his shoulder. With both hands on the plow handles he would urge Jack to action, "Now up, Jack," and the hinny stepped forward, the plow blades dug deep into the fallow soil, splitting a furrow of fresh moist black soil.

The animal near effortlessly moved forward. At the end of the row Jack paused while grandpa tipped the plow on its skid... "Gee Jack, up!" swinging right to cross over and pick up the next long row to be planted. To me it was an image straight out of Currier and Ives.

I would follow, kicking the large clumps of dirt to break them into smaller bits of friable earth to receive the seeds.

He laid out his particular plowing plan with the rows running East to West, so more light could penetrate between the plants and allowing the natural slope of the field towards the creek. He could irrigate the runoff water from the mountain across the road into the rows as he saw fit.

The pattern was interesting! They were basically squares overlapping from the downstream edge to the center of the field where he would turn right, repeat, repeat...repeat, telling the mule "gee," at every turn. The overlapping squares would soon have the whole field plowed, the wisdom behind such a pattern was that the animal and the plow being pulled behind would never have to make a sharp U-turn.

He told me that he had first seen a neighbor plow his farm in such a manner when he was a child. He was never too unbending not to learn from others, but had a stubborn streak in his own personality that put ol' Jack to shame. Like so many of his generation, being stubborn meant that he had to work it out on his own, but it made what he was doing much easier the next time.

Later on he purchased a small Ford Ferguson tractor, which made turning the soil much less a chore. But he always lamented that the tractor couldn't fertilize the ground... and it didn't know when to turn.

On planting day it was all hands. My mom, my grandparents' oldest child, and my older sister and myself would set about planting the seed for the corn, beans, squash and onion and tomato sets. Along the edge of the field we planted pumpkin and muskmelon. The harvest from that old field was always good, most likely because the backwaters would flood every spring bringing the silt and leaf compost downstream.

This was the cycle that mother nature had provided since the first fields were planted. Everything my grandpa knew was based upon the cycles of life... and verified by the farmers almanac.

The old farmers watched the sun's path through the sky. If the winds blew hard from the north in late winter and early spring, it most likely would be a good harvest in the fall. If, however, they blew from the Southwest, it was time to prepare for drought. In those days you saved and dried some of every bean and seed. The old timers would put up as many "cannin's" of vegetables and meat as possible, for that next lean winter.

When the leaves turned their bellies up, rain was soon to come, and when they dropped... it was time to water them. The folks down home paid close attention to everything that the plants and the sky told them.

Early mornings in late spring thru summer meant tending to plants, propping up branches heavy with fruit... and the incessant weeding. But it gifted us with a bountiful harvest. The sooner we got into the garden patch at home, the sooner we could get to my grandparents farm to work.

This allowed us to have much of the wonderful days of spring and summer to be kids and enjoy the bounty of life.

Come fall harvest, there was a flurry of activity up and down the holler. Neighbors helping neighbors was a rule. At my grandpa's farm there were two great black cast-iron caldrons in the fire pit. The canning jars were sanitized in one pot while the produce was prepared in the other. Two long canning tables were set up – on one all of the vegetables and fruit to be put up, and on the other boxes of jars on one end and towels laid on the other to cool the jars after they were filled. It was a genuine assembly line! Over the next few days this happened at friends and neighbors homes up and down the road. It was a unity that I have not seen since the days of my early youth, and that I long for today.

The jars of delicious nutrition were stored on the summer kitchen porch and behind chairs and under beds in the house, a mental note made by my grandmother, so she would know exactly where to go for the green beans, the corn or the potted meat.

The last great excitement of canning season was making jelly and apple butter. The air was delectable! I can still taste apple butter on fresh baked bread! You can't buy that kind of experience.

The final chores for a dirt farmer were to turn over the field and plant a fall crop for green fertilizer. Then to the shed to sharpen the plow and shovels, and to tend to the mule's needs for the winter. Later that meant to winterize the stinky ol' tractor.

That's what it was like being a dirt farmer and the memories that forever imprinted this author in a most rich way.

In our modern world we have lost touch of where our food comes from, and even the basic knowledge of growing and canning. The vast majority of our people today don't even know what it's like to dig potatoes, or to eat tomatoes, sun warmed, straight from the vine – and have scant respect for the earth that is provided all this for us.

Seasons come, and seasons go. The cycle of the earth is ever-changing, yet always the same... with hints of what is to come. There will be seasons of abundance and drought, periods of heat and cold. But nothing is new! It is all based in the endless cycles of this magic blue marble that we are so blessed to live upon.

My ancestors from here in America, and across the pond, have always been taught that we were the caretakers of the earth. Until recently this has been the way of life for all the peoples. Now many have forgotten our part in that balance, a lesson that we must re-learn.

Less we forget, that biblically we are the last thought of our Creator, not who we have conceived ourselves to be, e.g., the most important. We are not. For in this place where we live and work, we must live in Balance with all things. We are neither the masters of the earth nor its controller. We are but a microcosm upon our earth's skin that must learn to live within those parameters.

What will be left for our grandchildren will not be impacted by our relationship with the earth, but of the wisdom that we pass on that teaches them how to be a part of the whole.

- 9 -
Mrs. Tinker Taught Me to Trust

Grandma always took me to elementary school, and picked me up at the end of the day. Mom worked most weekdays and just wasn't available for the daily task. Usually Grandma drove me, sometimes she walked with me, but I always trusted she would be back when the day was done. She never let me down.

On the rare occasion my mom took me to school, the scene was not nearly so idyllic. Mom really wanted the experience of taking her little girl to school and being there to pick her up at the end of the day. I wanted it to! I was always excited to know mom would take me that day.

But as the time grew nearer, and the car approached the school, I would get a knot in my stomach, and panic would set in. I didn't want to get out of the car. I would cry, and beg. I just wanted to stay with mom. Hysteria would be an appropriate term.

Mom would assure me of her return. She would lovingly, but firmly, escort me to the door, but the tears came harder, and my pleas more desperate. My friends would come hold my hand, and try to get me to go into the school, but I was rarely mollified. On those days, I usually ended up going in at some point, but it was always a very traumatic thing for everyone involved.

I can't even imagine what my mother must have gone through. There were no obvious answers for why Grandma could take me without incident but my mom could not. I didn't understand it myself. At six years old, I had no explanation for what exactly made me panic, what I feared, and why it didn't happen with Grandma.

Mom was an RN and I found out later that she spoke with many colleagues during these days. It was upsetting to her, to put it mildly, to see me behave this way and to think she was the cause of it. We had a wonderful relationship and she couldn't bear to be a part of something causing me so much pain.

Eventually she found a child psychologist for me to see. She hoped it would expose the reason for the panic attacks and allow us both a way to resolve them.

The woman's name, as I knew it as a six year old, was Mrs. Tinker. She was very kind and easy to talk to. And I honestly thought that was all that was happening... she was a nice lady to talk to, and she had some pretty cool toys to play with while we chatted!

After quite some many visits, I was able to understand that my mother was not going to leave me at school and never come back. I also learned how to overcome the panic (one small experiment at a time), and that just because my dad "left me" – dying before I was born was neither his choice nor my fault – it did not mean my mom would do the same.

One step at a time, I learned to squelch the tears, keep a grip on myself, and walk into that school building. It was not fun. It was one of those things you would forever prefer not to ever have had to experience. First I fought hard to stay calm, failed a few times, got farther along every time we tried. And one day, I kissed her, said parting words, and got out of the car... walking in without incident.

A victory, at last. That's not to say I didn't have some setbacks. I did. But mom was forever patient and loving with me, Mrs. Tinker would talk through it with me, and I survived to fight another day, as the saying goes.

Emotional growth is a real challenge, at any age. I remember those days clearly, and that feeling of panic in the pit of my stomach sometimes returns. Eventually I learned it had a name, separation anxiety, and to be honest, I still struggle with it more than I'd like to admit.

Mom and I have lost a lot of loved ones in our lives. It's painful... and the scars it leaves run very deep. The sudden panic and terror that someone may not return from something as simple as a grocery run is something I'd rather live without. It truly doesn't add anything to my life in a positive way.

However, it is part of my life story, part of my experience. Mrs. Tinker was there when I needed someone other than my loving family to talk it out. She taught me to trust that not everyone is going to leave me.

When you have a deep seated fear, whatever the origin, it is something you live with, learn how to cope with if you're lucky, and it is also a growth point. Getting to the other side of anything unpleasant is a victory to be celebrated and something to bolster self-confidence.

Your fears need not control you. Only you control you. Never be afraid or embarrassed to ask for help when you need it. Let someone be there for you like Mrs. Tinker was for me.

These are crazy times to live in, the second decade of the twenty first century is no walk in the park. Make the best of it, take strength from your circle of family and friends, and learn to trust that you can make it through just fine.

Violet Rose Machovec Sabatka
Cerramar Beach Resort, Dorado, PR

- 10 -
Grandma Drank Too Much Sake

"Those poor little children! They have no clothes on... someone should cover them up! Give them something to wear!"

"Grandma, they're roman statues. Cherubs. They're not real."

"Well! Someone should put some clothes on them. The poor things, they must be cold!"

Caesar's Palace, Las Vegas, 1978. A family vacation. My mother, Aunt Marlene, my Grandma Violet, and me.

My grandmother Violet loved to play the slot machines. She had really been looking forward to this trip, a stopover on our way to Hawai'i that year. She had a brand new pacemaker, cutting edge technology in the late 1970s, and her energy was back in full swing.

Grandma loved to travel almost as much as she loved the slot machines. She was always "johnny on the spot" when my aunt and mom began planning the annual trip. Wherever they decided to go, Grandma was anxiously awaiting departure day, ready for a new adventure.

Our prior visit to Las Vegas was very short, and we had stayed at the MGM Grand. Grandma had always wanted to return and spend a few days so this was the year to do it. As Caesar's Palace was all the rage, Grandma had visions of Merv Griffin, Wayne Newton, and all the excitement of celebrity spotting.

During the evening in question, we had had dinner in the Japanese restaurant of the resort. A new experience for all of us. Teppanyaki. Dinner and a show all rolled into one! We'd never seen anything like it. Knives flying, food flipping through the air, so many courses and choices... and plenty of sake to go around.

I recall the little ceramic cups. And the small ceramic bottle. The liquid was warm, and had no bite or harsh flavor. Grandma was really enjoying it, believing that if it was just this small cup, and tasted so mild, she needn't worry about its effects.

Dinner went on and the meal was spectacular. Japanese food was new to all of us and we discovered we very much liked the foods and flavor combinations. We had yummy shrimp, and some delicious beef. There was rice, and so many vegetables in all colors of the rainbow. Onions, mushrooms, peppers, broccoli, carrots, a delicious dipping sauce. Everything was so fresh and bursting with excitement.

And throughout it all, Grandma was enjoying not only the food but the sake. Neither mom nor Aunt Marlene thought anything of it. Grandma didn't drink often and it tasted mild enough, so why have any concern?

It wasn't until the meal had ended and we noticed Grandma was happier than even her usual self. There was some giggling. Her wig had got a bit of a tilt to it. Her face was flushed. And her eyes were glassy.

When we all stood up to return to our rooms, it became clear that the mild tasting sake had done a number on Grandma. Not only was she very giggly, but she was a little unstable on her feet!

Mom got on one side of her, Aunt Marlene on the other, and we began our journey back to our hotel rooms. It seemed Grandma had had enough fun and probably needed to rest. The journey felt especially long that evening... what with Grandma becoming interested in all the shops' wares and all manner of sightseeing opportunities on the way through the hotel lobby, up the elevator and...

Including the poor little cherub statues who were barely clothed, lining the hallway leading to our hotel rooms!

That story has become one of my favorites. It was really funny, both then and now, but it is also poignant.

You see, not many days after we'd left Las Vegas and arrived on Maui for the second part of the vacation, Grandma had a massive stroke and died in an island hospital. It was an incredibly stressful and scary seven days, but she got her wish. It was something she'd been telling friends and family for a few years: That if she were to be able to choose a place to die, she couldn't think of anywhere more beautiful and perfect than Maui.

Up until that fateful moment in Lahaina, Grandma had had a fabulous vacation. She enjoyed herself immensely in Las Vegas. I can't recall whether she won any money but she sure did love those slot machines! She even tried her hand at Keno once or twice. We saw a few shows, which she really loved, and got to meet one of her favorites, Merv Griffin, outside the hotel. She'd had some time out at the pool on Maui, did some shopping, and enjoyed a few meals out.

Grandma Violet knew how to leave her day-to-day life at home, and how to embrace the excitement when she travelled. She made no excuses for living it up nor for laying low and relaxing.

Embrace every day as the gift that it is. Find the joy in not only the "big stuff," but in every detail and small blessing. Like Grandma Violet, we never know when our last opportunity will be to savor that last bite, linger in the warmth of a hug, or to say, "I love you" to someone special.

Carpe Diem. Live every day like it's your last.

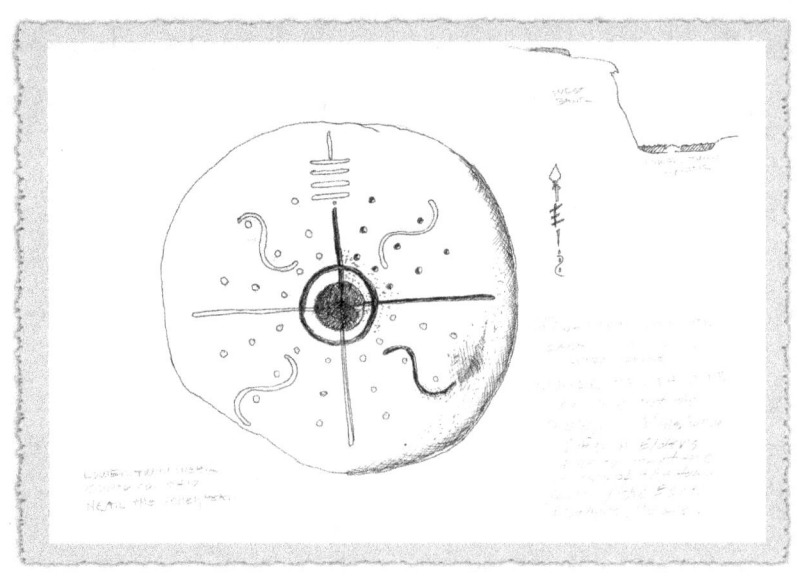

The Old Altar Stone
Original Artwork by Jim Great Elk Waters

- 11 -

The Vanishing Altar Stone

It's most strange how so many of the buildings and other items of importance seem to just disappear as we grow older. Take for example, the home of my formative years in southern Ohio. It's not the memories that disappear but the physical building. Today there is nothing more than an empty lot with a few stones that were the front porch, horse mounting stone and the stone slab walkway in the front. The house and barn, wrought iron fence, the cherry tree – even the three hole outhouse – all gone, and vanished in the rubble. Likewise, my father's parents' home and business all gone, now replaced by a cemetery. General stores, tobacco warehouses, and covered bridges no longer exist except in my fading memory.

With broom in hand, the giant hands of progress and abandonment relentlessly sweep away all things man-made. It seems as if humankind has little need or desire for things temporary. Even those made of stone are often ground back into gravel and sand to start their journey again.

"Even the hardest stone mountain will become dust. Nothing lasts except memories shared from mouth to ear." - The Code of Oral Traditions, Mide'way philosophy.

Permit me to share a story about a very particular stone that existed long before the time of my youth. Created and used as the cultural center of my ancestors centuries ago, it was the ceremonial Altar Stone of my American Indian ancestors, the Mide'wiian People of the Panji Seppe Earth Culture. I have been taught by my Elders, mouth to ear, that our people have always lived in this area that we today know as Blue Creek. And that our culture and traditions are those of our ancestors who were the people who worked with the stone and the earth and the water to honor the Creator that caused us all to be.

Anthropologists and archaeologists have, for over two centuries, attempted to define my ancestors only by the relics and remnants that were left behind. We have been named by different scientists in different decades as the Mound Builders, the Hopewell people, the Fort Ancient people, and just prehistoric Indians. All this without ever hearing a single word uttered by the people themselves. In fact, the professionals have absolutely rejected any possibility that there might be surviving descendants of those people.

Isn't it most quixotic of them to assume that they, by the deciphering of their "runes," could define whole groups of people... without any knowledge of how they thought, lived and practiced their faith? Such is the religion of the Church of Anthropology

Please do not get me wrong, their research and documentation *have* been of great value and importance in helping us, the descendants of these people, to understand the remnants of the physical attributes as they relate to the Sacred Oral Traditions passed down to us.

As our ancestors faced invasions of not only Europeans, but other nation building tribes who swept into our homelands, our Elders were forced to leave behind our Sacred Ceremonial items too large to carry.

One such very large ceremonial item of our past is now missing.

This was a very large altar stone that once rested on the western bluffs of the headwaters of Lower Twin Creek... overlooking the vast valley south. This ancient box canyon created by the glacier melts thousands of year before, was only accessible from the south until the first settlers in the area discovered this beauty. Wanting an access from the north, they carved a rudimentary road up the face of the ancient crumbling layers of the sandstone cliff.

For centuries this hidden Valley was home to the keepers of the faith. It is here they created, upon the face of a large flat stone, an altar where Mide' ceremonies were held. One could envision the gathering upon the flat bluff above the creek, Elders and medicine people practicing ancient beliefs in the seclusion of the deep valley.

If you listened closely you could still hear the rhythms, and the chants, and the reverent words spoken in a long ago forgotten language

As a child under the tutelage of my Elders, the Mide', who were the carriers of the pipe, the keepers of our culture, I was gifted with the obligation to memorize and pass on the tenants of our faith.

The principle belief held sacrosanct was learning, understanding.

Our ancient traditional religion – that we know to be the Mide'Way – is the study and understanding of the four levels of the Earth and Sky... that we may respectfully understand the great gifts of our Creator. On the surface the premise is similar to the Midewiwin faith of our Anishinaabe cousins, but it is vastly different in many other ways. It is possible that both religions originated from our shared Algonquian tribal core. We will never know.

As part of my learning of the rituals required, I was taken to the altar stone by one of my elder Mide'. We had traveled near the full length of the road along the creek until we were close to the bluffs that defined the headwaters of the creek. After we parked, we took a couple of shovels and brooms from the back of the car and crossed the shallow creek. My Mide' walked directly towards the sheer face of the wall on the far side of the creek. It looked insurmountable, but with just a slight move sideways, a near invisible crevice appeared in the wall.

Covered with leaves and earth, were ancient steps... stones placed to the right and left like a Swedish ladder, that made the ascent easy. Taking a few steps onto the flat area of the bluff, using our shovels, we removed accumulated soil and leaves. In the place that had been covered by that shallow layer, now laying bare, the ancient sacred altar was revealed.

It was a flat stone nearly seven foot round with images and lines carved into its surface. In the center was a deeper carving, a depression of about two feet in diameter and nearly six inches deep. The first time I saw the altar stone I was speechless. As a pre-teen I could have laid on the stone with outstretched arms and legs – much as Leonardo da Vinci's circle of man drawing – and my hands nor my feet would extend beyond the stone's edge. It was spectacularly large.

Clearing out the remnants of the earth in the depression, we started a small ceremonial fire in the old way, and as we sat on the stone I was taught the meanings and stories of the various markings and carvings.

It is important to note that the religion of my people is not one that is subject to evangelism, but that which was taught to those who are related by blood to the People of the Panji Seppe Naube. The specifics of the teaching are only for those descended within this group.

I will share with you however, some of the carvings on the stone.

On the areas both to the north and south of the ceremonial fire pit were four straight parallel lines radiating from the center representing the studies of the four levels of the Earth and Sky. Above and below were symbols of our Deity. There were other carvings that were like a table of contents in a book... Notes to remind us of what is in the individual chapters.

The Stone and the Comet Mound were the places of my annual pilgrimage to study with my Mide', until I joined the United States Navy. Periodically later, during visits to my family in Ohio, I again went to the source of our Way, to reaffirm my spiritual values.

For the next three decades of my life, I lived mostly in southern California. There, like most young men, I grew away from my childhood teachings and embraced those of the world. Gut deep, I still had a longing for the old places and those of my teachings. All the while I continued to practice my spirituality, sharing by example the basics of being a man Born from the Earth. As a spiritual Pipe Carrier for my People I was often asked to speak on subjects of Native American history and spirituality.

Often the light of the Mide' Lodge's four rooms dimmed, but it was never extinguished. Some thirty years later I returned to the place of the stone altar to find everything changed.

During my absence a one hundred year deluge had destroyed the creek bed below. Modern engineers surveyed the area and determined that there was nothing to hinder another disastrous flood in the valley. It was decided that the small creek that had once meandered back-and-forth across the valley, whose spring rains flooded the lower valley, would better serve the area as a mostly straight watershed. Soon giant earth moving equipment came in and created a creek bed that would better control future flooding.

Because of the Great Lower Twin Creek flood and the erosion that followed, and the mechanical realigning of the creek bed... the bluff that had held the sacred altar stone for millennia had disappeared. No remnant of it remained. I spent several days walking up and down the creek, from the old bluff – much smaller now – south a few hundred yards searching for any bit or piece of the stone.

I found no trace. It is possible that the bluff had given way, tipping the stone into the creek below... face down. At that point it would have looked like any other large slab of bedrock.

The altar stone had vanished.

In truth, I am the mirror image of an anthropologist. I have no artifact to study, but I do have the ancient teachings in our oral tradition whereas they have artifacts without the knowledge of the secret to why the artifacts were created in the beginning. They guess, I know.

Since that time I've used my small portable altar stone, made of the same rocks as the original, to practice my religion. It has done me well all these years. I do long for the times when I sat and listened to the Elders as they would teach me the Ways of our ancestors. Like a sponge, I willingly soaked it all in.

Now I am the Elder, teaching our ancient pathway of our spirituality... to a chosen few.

This experience reinforced the admonition that we must never let the people die. When I first heard those words as a child, I thought it meant never letting the elderly in our family to die. Of course, that is an impossibility. Once while sitting with one of my teachers, a beloved aunt, she explained it in a way that I understood clearly. It simply meant that we should never allow our culture, traditions, ceremonies and spirituality die. It is our obligation, our job to ensure that the path created before, by the ancestors, should never be forgotten... And that it be passed on to future generations, mouth to ear.

This is why it is so important that each of us write down the stories that were told to us by our Grandparents and the Elders. When the words die, never to be read or spoken again... It is then that the people die.

– 12 –
"Remember when...?"

"There was that one time that Helen decided she wanted to smell all the cologne at the perfume counter. She sprayed each of her wrists, and then each of her forearms, then her elbows... and then she wanted me to stand there so she could spray me, too! At the end, she sprayed her knees and she was dancing around the floor trying to smell them. When she figured out she couldn't, she wanted to spray mine! ‹raucous laughter on both ends of the phone lines› Carl came along and couldn't understand what the heck we were doing smelling each other's knees!! ‹more laughter›"

This is one of my sister Diane's favorite stories to tell about our sister Helen who died some time ago. She laughs so hard she can barely get through it and then I start laughing too. And we end with a great smile because we just brought our sister back to us, even if just for a few minutes.

Grief and grieving comes in all shapes, sizes, and colors. No two people grieve exactly the same way. Some have lost many people in their lives, some have been fortunate enough to have lost none or very few.

The single commonality is that everyone grieves differently. And however they do it, is just perfect for them. Some suffer quietly. Some explode with grief and anger. Some must keep "telling the story," repeatedly – to everyone and anyone who will listen – as they work their way through the shock and pain. (And there is always shock... even when we think we are prepared for someone's passing, the reality of the loss is always surprising.)

Some grieving happens with the need to tell stories about the person. To many, story telling brings peace and promotes healing. Another family member or friend who knew them, and can tell their own stories about them, are of great comfort during this time. Hours may be spent over days and months telling stories of the wonderful parts of the person and what they meant to us.

In my family, we recall the crazy, outrageous, stories from a person's life. "Remember when..." is a common opening line to our memories.

Every story we tell brings those lost closer to the veil, through which we can almost see them, almost reach out to them and touch them once again. Many of the stories you are reading in this book are those stories. And there are countless more. They keep my loved ones alive and vibrant, and as close to me as the smile and laugh they bring.

So many wonderful memories. Keep them vibrant. It's a way of never letting them stray too far.

Memories give your loved ones eternal life. Death doesn't kill your recollections and stories, nor the feelings of closeness when you relive them.

Recognize the stories you tell amongst your friends and family as love, respect, and a yearning to be reunited. It's healthy. It's cathartic. It warms the heart and heals the soul.

Don't shy from grief or the fear of feeling the pain of loss. Tell the stories. Look at the photos. Let your other family and friends know who this person was and why they were so special to you.

Your children can only know them from your stories. And others in your life similarly. Love them, past and present. Tell about your memories and share the laughter. By doing so you allow your love to bridge the gap of time.

- 13 -
The Indian School Incident

This is a story of an extraordinary adventure gone awry.

Recently, I visited the Heard Museum in Phoenix to explore the galleries of Native American art and history of the Southwest Indians. Many of the exhibits were poignant, educational and inspiring. I was particularly drawn to the gallery on government Indian Schools because of my personal connection.

Their contemporary exhibit however, was most disappointing, as it was very politicized. It showed our People as victims – this is as far from the truth and possible. Europeans and later Americans did, in fact, take the homelands from the many people who first inhabited what is now the United States and Canada. In a massive attempt, the federal government desperately attempted to "civilize" the indigenous people.

However... They only partially succeeded in limiting our languages, cultures and traditions that are returning strong today. Although they have succeeded in making some of our people dependent on government charity, the many Tribes, organizations and familial groups of First Peoples are actively teaching the heritage that was once thought lost. Throughout the time of assimilation and to this day, the Elders, storytellers and medicine people have retained that which make us – the 500 plus nations of indigenous entities – uniquely American Indian.

We were never victims, nor have we thought ourselves such. I personally have only met a few First People who believe they are victims of America's sad historic cultural ethnic cleansing. This is a sobering footnote of the group-think of some, but it doesn't reflect the exemplary positive lives and the extraordinary achievements of many of our people today.

Exploring their Indian School exhibit prompted me to remember what happened one fateful week to my dad, Chief Ten Moons Watters, and about his childhood Incident in a Northwest Territory Indian School.

My dad was born in the fall of 1904, in the small town of Portsmouth, Ohio. He was the second son of a truly entrepreneurial couple. His father was a crack salesman and sometimes-con-artist. The folks around the region oft said, "He could sell a fur coat to a grizzly bear." He always had a new scheme to make his millions. His mother Ma Jessie was an alpha female, a cunning business woman, an adventuress, hard when necessary and soft as a down pillow to those in need.

Here is where the story begins.

Sometime around the end of the first decade of the last century, my grandfather "Big Dad" Watters set out on a journey to the west – "fer piece" from his home in Appalachian Ohio. As a representative of a major shoe company (this was his current get-rich concept), his job was to open new markets in the old Northwest Territory that stretched as far west as Minnesota. His job was to stop at general stores, blacksmiths and cobblers shops in the towns along the way to sell his wares. His sample kit had all the shoes his company offered and with a convincing "silver tongue" he would make contracts to have selections of products delivered to those new accounts.

This was in the time before most people had automobiles. So my grandfather took his old freight wagon, and converted it to what today we call an RV. I was never told what it looked like but, if it were representative of other traveling salesman's wagons, it was horse drawn and had flat sides and a flat roof, with a fold out shelf for cooking. Inside were the sleeping accommodations, as well the salesman samples and kits.

It must've been quite a sight. In it was everything one would need to be self-sufficient on the dirt roads, through forest and across the vast prairies of this newly developing wonderful land we call America. What made this trip extraordinarily special was that he took his youngest son Jim with him on this great journey.

What I know of this event was shared with me by my father.

For most of my life dad never shared stories that had to do with our Indian heritage, in fact he never admitted being Native American – specifically Shawnee – until the seventh decade of his life. I learned then that he was actually ashamed because he had denied his heritage, out of his great fear of being forced onto the reservations in the Oklahoma Indian Territory… now the State of Oklahoma.

While stopping in a small town in Minnesota, my grandfather heard there was an Indian School in the vicinity. He thought that it would be good for his son to be placed there temporarily to gain additional schooling, and to be with his "own kind." This would also allow my grandfather to concentrate on sales in the area.

Big Dad dropped off my dad at the school the following Monday – with the promise to return at the end of the week, to gather him up for the trip back home.

With that, my grandfather went on his way.

Fast forward to the mid 1970's, and how I learned the rest of the story I am about to share with you. I was visiting my parents down at their place on Rocky Fork Lake. Dad and I sought out a bit of shade under a giant oak down by the lakes edge to chew the fat. We both were fond of occasionally smoking a pipe while reminiscing. This was one of those special times.

As I recall, dad began this way, "Long ago now, when I was a little shaver, I went with my pa on a sellin' trip out west." He continued, "This is what happened on my first day at the Indian school in Minnesota."

He paused as if to remember more clearly, took a puff on his pipe, and continued. "Right off the teacher was real friendly welcoming me into the class and all."

Hoping to fit in with all the other Indian kids, "I respectfully said, 'Miigwich' [thank you in our Algonquian dialect], and suddenly all hell broke out."

Unbeknownst to him, speaking a native language in that school was forbidden, subject to strong discipline.

"Well now, she yanked me by the arm to the front of the class, where she cut my long hair with her big scissors, and dragged me to a closet at the back of the room. She shoved me into the dark little room and locked me in." My dad wasn't prone to being fearful, but this had his attention. What was going to happen next?

He continued retelling the events that day.

"Later that morning when the food was brought for the rest of the class, I was given a large porcelain pail with my food in it, meat stew and bread, real tasty. Oh, and there was a clay jug of water."

He soon found the same pail that had his food in it was also to be used for his toilet. They told him it was washed daily... hopefully with soap.

"You could hear the classes, each grade, reciting their work and listening to the teacher's lectures," he said. Through the door of his closet prison my dad applied himself to learning the lessons at hand. He wanted to learn what the teacher had to share. Early in the week he had been given paper and a pencil with which he took notes.

My dad's mind was like a sponge, always thirsty for more knowledge. Throughout his life he never quit "brain stuffing." All my siblings have exceptional IQ's, and pop must have been a borderline genius. It is important to note that my family on both sides have been blessed with generations of parents who taught them the basics of education even before they began formal schooling.

"From that first day, I was never let out of the closet." He continued, "I slept on an old blanket and wrapped up in my long coat. I got used to the dark and the door being loose fit, allowed rays of light in." He stated, "I didn't like it one bit, but I was getting used to my prison."

Indian School Dormitory

On Friday his father returned as promised, to see how his son was doing. On entering the classroom and not seeing his boy, he asked the teacher were his Jim was. Arrogantly, the teacher pointed to the closet in the back of the room and said, "He's in there, being punished."

My grandfather was never a man to be trifled with, and he held family sacred. I don't know how the teacher lived, for my grandfather had shot and killed more than one person in his life. I can only imagine the rage, anger, hate and desire to do extreme violence upon this person. But as dad shared what he had heard through the door, "My father quietly said, open the door and let my son out. We're going home."

The teacher made some reply and then my dad heard a gasp from the kids in the room.

Footsteps approached and a key turned in the lock... the door opened.

As his eyes adjusted to the bright light in the room he saw his father – all six foot two inches of him – standing erect with a pistol pointed at the head of the teacher. "Come on son, we're going back home," his father said quietly. He took the papers with his notes, leaving the pencil on the floor, and they walked out the door... Big Dad still holding the pistol in his hand.

Dad said that a lot of things happened in a hurry. They mounted the wagon – hearing the school bell ringing an alarm – his father whipped the horse to a fast run. For miles they rushed eastward until darkness closed. They made cold camps for the next three nights, until they thought they were far enough east that they were certain no one was following. They returned home and told no one of the incident.

Some months later the sheriff came to my grandparents home and told them that the feds had a warrant out for my grandfather's arrest. Living in rural Appalachia, I am certain that the local sheriff simply told the agents that he hadn't seen my grandfather for sometime. He probably said, "They all got up and left." The locals thereabouts had no truck with the federal government interfering with the good folk in our hills.

I asked my dad if he recalled what his father said about the whole incident, and he replied, "My father uttered, 'G-d damn their souls to Hell.'"

Big Dad never forgave the school, nor himself for putting his child in such danger.

I would think that this experience would have jaded my father on education. To the contrary, my dad went on to garner an extraordinary wealth of knowledge. Graduating from high school, he went on to college in Ohio achieving a two-year college degree in Medicine and then to a college in West Virginia graduating with a degree in Engineering. He was remarkably educated, speaking and reading nine different languages including most of the romance tongues as well as Mandarin Chinese and Yiddish/Hebrew. He never quit learning, bringing home books and magazines, consuming them with the ferocity of a ravenous animal.

When he passed on in his late 80s, the lights had dimmed, but in the recesses of his computer-like mind, you knew he was still learning.

Our family's story is but one of thousands upon thousands of American Indian histories marred by the Colonists' concept of assimilation. This seemed to be a universal attitude towards the indigenous – enslave them in the concentration camps "fondly called" reservations.

They did divide us, between families and friends – those who had been placed "under federal protection" and the millions today who can document their Tribal heritage, but are ineligible to be recognized as such because of laws. And one wonders why the people in Appalachia have a deeply rooted distrust of the Federal Government.

The reducing of the individual rich heritages and cultures to the lowest common denominator would seen to have been inevitable… to the contrary, Wisdom Keepers, Elders and storytellers have preserved this extraordinary heritage for the individual descendants and the world at large.

Notable cultural preservationists such as Zora Neale Hurston's epics including "Barracoon" that documented the story of "Cudjo Lewis," the final slave-ship survivor, and her collection of folklore, "Mules and Men," are beyond enlightening. Another is Doctor Lily Penleric's brilliant work "Songcatcher," that recorded and preserved the music of early rural America. This is but a short list of First Peoples of the Great Turtle Island (America) authors. For further readings on these matters, please explore the writings of Sherman Alexie, Paula Gunn Allen, Professor Duane Niatum, Charles Eastman, John Joseph Mathews…and so many more.

The history of assimilation and the attempted ethnic cleansing of our First People's language, cultures and traditions is a most morbid part of our history. But…we were never… nor will we ever be victims.

- 14 -
Indian Time

"We're supposed to be there at 1:00 and the GPS is saying we won't arrive until 1:30! We're going to be late!"

"It'll be fine."

"But... what happens if we walk in a half hour late?!"

"It'll be fine."

"But... I'm not even going to have time to change! You told me to wear shorts and they're in the back seat!"

"Change in the car along the way. It's a rural road. It'll be fine."

"But... how's that going to look when we come barreling in a half hour late?!"

"Look, relax! Ceremony never starts on time anyway, people straggle in a half hour, even an hour late sometimes. It just is. They know we're coming. They won't start until everyone is there. It's a beautiful drive, on a beautiful day. Relax, you're on Indian Time now."

"What's Indian Time?"

And so went the conversation on the drive to my first tribal ceremony in western Ohio. Jim was driving and I was frantically watching the clock and the map. The thought of being late for my first time participating in ceremony, with people I'd only met once before, was seriously stressing me out.

I was already walking into a very new experience, one I had hoped to realize most of my life, and it was nerve-wracking in itself. But then to be late! What would they think of us? Of me? Would they be insulted? Would they start without us and I would make a spectacle of an interruption? Would we be banned from entry?

As I remember back to that now, almost seven years to the day, I just have to chuckle. I know what I was thinking but... what was I *thinking*?

The People of Oshawanodasse would never give it a second thought that anyone was half an hour late. They don't adhere to such strict limitations of the clock during tribal time as is necessitated during the work week. On those weekends of gathering, they are far too busy catching up with one another, fussing over the communal meal, readying the Great House, tending the lodge fire, and watching the children run around playing and laughing. Time doesn't exist by the clock on The Land. It is merely a series of memories-in-the-making, laughter, story-telling, and teaching. The sun is high in the sky, it is setting, or it is replaced by the moon. That's it. It's not about hours and minutes, it's about the *day*.

In October 2013, I had no concept of "Indian Time" but I trusted Jim, who'd been a part of these people for over thirty years. If anyone knew them, it was he. And so I did my best to follow his counsel and enjoy the beautiful sunny fall day and the ride through western Ohio farm country.

As it turned out, that drive was to be one of countless ones, through all four seasons, for several years. The People came to be *my* people, my family by affection. Sisters and brothers, and elders, all whom I've grown to love deeply, respect, and trust.

Eventually, I no longer worried much about our arrival for gathering days. I knew we'd get there in plenty of time for the ceremony and festivities. No one ever started without us. I knew it would always be fine. On rare occasions when we really were running late, even by Indian Time, I could always text a tribal sister to let her know where we were and when we'd be there. Per Jim's advice those years ago, it was never an issue in any way. The clock was for coming together, not for dividing those who got there on time from those who didn't. If you were there with a loving heart, you were there on time.

Fast forward to the Era of Zoom. We are now living in Arizona while everyone else is still in Ohio. We've not been able to return for ceremony but we still come together once a month via the magic of internet connections. Still, nothing has changed with respect to the concept of time.

"We're waiting for so-and-so. They said they might be a little late."

"Oh ok," everyone says together.

And the chit chat continues.

"I wonder where so-and-so is... let me text them."

And the chitchat continues.

"Oh, hi so-and-so! Really glad you're here! How are you? How's your family? How was the drive home?"

And the beat goes on, as the saying goes.

I am a person who is instinctually driven by time. By way of nurture, I also tend to be driven by the clock. But...

Time and the clock are not the same things.

I'll give you as long as you need to ponder that, all I ask is that you don't dismiss it outright as crazy talk.

Think about it. I'll wait.

Welcome back.

What do you think about that concept? What makes you think that time and the clock are synonymous?

"Oooh, ooh! Pick me, pick me! I have the answer!!"

It's because that's what someone taught you as a kid when you were learning about responsibility and how to be somewhere "on time."

Whose time?

Yours? Theirs? The Universe?

The Clock is an agreed upon representation of time. It is not time itself. We get so wrapped up in running our lives by the clock that we forget it's only a manmade conglomeration of gears and springs, or batteries and quartz crystals.

For eons, we have been tracking time, but only in terms of years, seasons, and moons. It was not until recently (the last 300 years), with the advent of pendulum clocks, that we began precisely tracking hours, minutes, and seconds.

Agrarian societies benefited most from knowing the seasons – when to plant and harvest. When the days were longest and shortest. When the moon would be full. Little else mattered to them.

Religious communities needed to know when to gather for prayers and services, and were therefore some of the most renowned clockmakers.

Later as national and world economies grew, precise time tracking was necessary. The pendulum clock was perfected in the 1700s and in the 1920s, the quartz timepiece first saw the light of day (forgive the pun).

Use the clock as a tool for those events that require such precision, but respect time as something set aside from the ticking and clicking of gears.

When we are with the ones we love, the clock is not the dictator, only the beating of our hearts. That is why when we are close with loved ones – as a baby and mother, or a close family unit – our heartbeats sync with one another. We become one entity through the rhythm of the human drumbeat.

Be wary of how much you restrict the joy in your life, and the vision of your own happiness, with a manmade device. We are divine beings, governed by the heavenly bodies of the Universe. Choose wisely when to watch the clock, and when to listen to a more natural and organic rhythm.

– 15 –
Pies Like Grandma Used to Make

As a youngster, I just loved to be with my grandparents and elders, for they told stories and... well, just spoiled me rotten. I tried to spend as much time "down at the store" with my grandparents, aunts, uncles and other family members as they would have time to share. Those days with my Elders were the well source that defined who I am today. To sit at the knee of an Elder is liken to attending classes at Oxford or Cambridge. These invaluable resources passed on our history. We are but the caretakers of such narratives, and are responsible for passing the torch to others

The food and company was always great at Jimmie's Place. Neighbors and strangers alike would stop in for a cup of coffee, ice cold soda pop or to enjoy a bite to eat. The "store" was actually a restaurant, gas pumps and tourist cabins along the old main east-west route – US Route 52.

This was the hub of the area for locals and travelers alike. Jimmie's Place was located at the top of the Ferry Lane in Sandy Springs, Ohio, just 3 miles west of the village of Buena Vista. The lane appropriately named because it led to the river ferry that connected Kentucky with Ohio. The demographics on either side of the Ohio River in that area didn't warrant the construction of a bridge, so the ferry was vitally important.

To some of the locals on the Ohio side, this was a vital connection to the outside world because Green Township was, and still is, "dry." This meant that if you wanted an adult libation other than moonshine, you would have to go to Kentucky to buy a good Bourbon. Vanceburg was also the closest location for dry-goods and department stores.

Without a doubt as many people traveled north for the food and companionship at Jimmie's Place, as did those taking the ferry south for other wares.

In fact, people traveling from Cincinnati, Ohio eastward, and Huntington, West Virginia westward, as well as those taking the ferry between Ohio and Kentucky all passed by Jimmie's Place.

Built in the 1920's by my dad and family members, Jimmie's Place was known for great food, good conversation and hot coffee. The restaurant itself was a combination eatery, local place to buy notions, small grocery goods and a World War I, World War II and Korean War military museum.

On a narrow shelf running around the main room of the restaurant were trophies from wars past, local artifacts and bits and pieces of great interest. On the wall one would also find African safari trophy animals, looking as if they had just pushed through the wall itself. They often astounded, and sometimes even frightened, some visitors upon first seeing the Zulu Warrior's ceremonial headdress that featured an African lion mane, or the mounted heads of a Kudo or water buffalo.

Military arm patches and insignias were stapled on the wall behind the shelf and were always an inspiration for patriots, those with military connections. They invited comments from guests about other family members that were in this unit or that.

The "southwest room" was so named because it was decorated with murals portraying New Mexico and Arizona scenes from the 1920's and 30's. It was complete with sombreros, cactus and serapes – mementos of family trips "out west." It was a special place to dine.

During cooler days, the warm morning stove in the center of the room was the place to huddle and warm up. During the summer months, however, the large Coca-Cola ice chest was a place to grab your favorite beverage. My grandfather Big Dad would always remind you if you were dallying too long, putting your hands in the ice cold water. "That's enough!"

The main draw at Jimmie's Place was the good food – locally sourced when available and of the best quality always. My grandparents would never serve a meal to a stranger that they wouldn't serve to their own parents. Their pride showed.

Jimmie's Place
Original Artwork by Jim Great Elk Waters

Knowing the value of advertising, we took good advantage of signage all along the front of the building, and with large roadway signs at either end of the parking lots. Signs urging you to "drink Coca-Cola" or stop in for "Tasty Eats." "Stop for a Meal," "Good Gulf Gas," and "Stay for the evening. Clean cabins and fresh pressed linens." Anything to entice travelers to stop for a while.

Did I mention good food?

For many years after its heyday, I would meet people who had stopped at Jimmie's Place. Their first comments were, "the food was great," or "I had the best meal ever there!"

I enjoyed working with family members preparing food for our guests. I did chores as needed in the kitchen – peeling potatoes, chopping salad and washing dishes. Along with the other members of our family, I waited tables. I was too young to take orders but I filled coffee, brought out ice water and soda pop, made sure that there was bread or biscuits or crackers on the table. After the guests had left I cleaned the table, putting the dishes in a gallon pail, and food scraps in another. We kept the scraps for Big Dad's dog or for the neighbors to feed their pigs. In reality, there was rarely anything left over.

What I enjoyed the very most was helping to cook. Everything from standing on a stool and flipping burgers, to making cold cut sandwiches, and anything else that they would let me try my hand at.

Speaking of hands, I really liked to help make pies, which we usually did on weekends. The pies were always a favorite of everyone's. Hot apple pie or any other fruit that was in season, served with a big dollop of Ideal ice cream. In the fall pumpkin pies were in order. My grandfather would ask me to make the pie dough, which I learned later was because my small hands couldn't knead the dough enough to make it tough.

I would take each ball of dough and roll it out to about a quarter inch thickness, schmear a bit of butter on 1/2 and fold it over and then roll it out the other direction. I repeated the process four times. That always made for a nice flaky crust. That was the way Ma Jessie always wanted it made. After kneading the dough and chilling it in the fridge, I would roll it out and drop it into pie tins. A secret I learned from my uncle Bill was to grease the pan with bacon fat before I put in the dough. This always caused the crust to crisp on the bottom and outside but stay light and fluffy.

Being at Jimmie's Place, for a meal or a cold drink, or to help my family's enterprise, was as much of a treat for this little fella as it was for any visitor who would come to the door. Jimmie's Place was always an experience. When the bells jingled on the door they announced another customer entering. They would always be greeted with, "Welcome neighbor! Come on in and set a spell!"

For most of my adult life anytime I mentioned our family's restaurant down in Sandy Springs, many would gush at length telling about their experience and how much they enjoyed their visits. It was a general feeling that they missed the old place... Not nearly as much as I did though.

Oh yes, remember when I spoke of the advertising all around the building and all the billboards? One of the most memorable signs that people recalled was the one that read, "Fresh Hot Pies, Like Grandma Used to Make!"

If they only knew!

- 16 -
Tuesday Nights at Kiddie Park

Mom had every other Tuesday off from work. Tuesday off, especially in the summer time, meant we could spend the late afternoon and evening together, doing something "fun."

Fun to me has always been amusement parks. I get it from my mother (see the story *Rollercoasters and Death Drops* elsewhere in this book). As soon as I was old enough, she began taking me to Memphis Kiddie Park in Brooklyn, Ohio.

Built in 1952, it (still) has about ten rides, including a steel rollercoaster (the Little Dipper) specially designed for kids that also happens to be the oldest continuously operated steel coaster in North America. There is a miniature golf course attached as well. And right next to the parking lot a *fabulous* grass covered hill perfect for rolling down! I know this because mom indulged me often, joining me on the dizzying twirl down the hill and then racing back up to the top.

Less than half an hour drive from our home in Slavic Village, Memphis Kiddie Park was a summertime staple. We spent many Tuesday evenings there, me running from ride to ride and mom keeping a close eye on me. The smell of cotton candy, gear grease from the rides, and fresh mown summer grass are readily recalled almost fifty years later.

As a child, the rides were perfectly sized and approachable. I loved the hand cars where I would furiously pump my arms to propel myself forward on the rail, oftentimes getting tired out, slowing down, and told to "hurry up already!" by some impatient kid behind me. I remember riding the carousel with mom, usually on horses that would go up and down as we went round and round.

But my favorite of all time were the cars that spun and spun. The faster they spun, the more I would laugh. "Faster! Faster, mom!

Spin faster!" I would yell as she jumped forward to spin the car faster as I went by. And then the uncontrollable giggling and laughter as I flung myself this way and that trying to get it to spin faster still. It was my favorite and I loved to jump back in line and go all over again.

The Little Dipper steel coaster was just my size, and just my speed. It was scary and fun all at the same time. The thrill of climbing the first hill was heady, and then the mild slopes thereafter were just enough to be fun without the terrifying part. It was slow enough that below the tracks you could see the little motorized race cars zipping around the track, weaving in and out of the coaster structure.

Cotton candy was always a must. I don't recall there being flavors as we have today. It was a big pink fluff of sticky sweet goodness spun onto a paper straw/stick. I loved it! It was magic that something so big and puffy could dissolve in my mouth in an instant. I remember the crunch of the sugar when I pulled off big bites.

Sometimes we got hot dogs or burgers for dinner from the food stand where the cotton candy was. But most often, after the park, it was a trip to McDonald's for a burger and fries that was the coup de grace on the excitement for the evening.

At that time, McDonalds had no dine in option. It was two golden arches, a walk up counter and that was it. You ordered your food and either ate at a picnic table out front or in the car.

In 1972, you could get a cheeseburger, fries, apple pie and coke for about $1 – total. Sometimes we'd get a fish sandwich. The Big Mac was new, only five years old, and the Quarter Pounder had only been introduced the year before. The fries were still cooked in beef lard, a flavor my generation will never forget, and many of us still pine for in this age of unsaturated vegetable cooking fat.

We would come back to the car and eat our burgers and fries. We would talk about everything and anything that was on my mind that evening... which was usually tons. Mom still chides me about how many questions I asked as a child. There was never a shortage of conversation, as I recall.

By the time we finished eating, it would be dark, I'd be getting sleepy, and mom would drive us home.

Those Tuesday evenings with her hold such fond memories. It was mother-daughter time when we were able to be silly, talk about serious things, and just catch up on "stuff" together. It was a way to detach from the rest of the household and it made me feel loved and special.

Take time with someone(s) you hold most dear.

My mother showed me, during these evenings, that despite the hectic schedule in the household (between her work, my school, and extracurricular activities), I was important enough to set aside an entire evening. Every week. Without exception. She made it a priority and therefore made me *a priority.*

Whether your children, your spouse, a best friend, or an elder, when you set time aside just for them, it is impactful beyond words.

Today is a very different world than it was in the early 1970s. We have so many more things pulling at our time and so many more ways to be distracted and entertained. They are actually ways to be in solitude, not necessarily ways to be with those we love.

We must be aware, every day, that families and friends are the core of our existence. No one exists in a vacuum. Relationships, both early and mature, must be doted on and kept special amongst all other aspects of our busy and frantic lives.

My mother's time with me helped shaped my vision of what family means. These gifts are priceless. Your loved ones' vision of themselves, both now and in the future, will also be shaped by the part of yourself you share with them.

The Golden Age of Rail Travel

- 17 -
I Love Riding the Rails

I grew up listening to the adults in my family talking about riding on trains to go anywhere beyond their local area. Following World War I, which was fresh in the minds of my parents and grandparents – who marveled at the tremendous changes made during that period of time – riding the rails was an extraordinary adventure. They spoke of taking the "local" from Portsmouth to Cincinnati for a day of shopping, or upriver to Huntington, West Virginia to visit family. They spoke of the old Pullman accommodations aboard the coach cars, and sleepers for overnight excursions to the East Coast. They marveled at the comfort and the speed of train riding, so unlike driving their cars on the rough roads that were the norm before the interstate system was put in place in the early 1950s.

The highlight for most of them was eating on board. The food was scrumptious, freshly prepared just as if they'd gone into a five star restaurant such as the Delmonte in New York. Sitting at a table for four, presented with lemons (an exotic fruit in that day), china and silver, was such a treat... All the time watching the country pass by the windows.

All of this chatter by my seniors, while I would sit quietly listening to them, imprinted me forever. I couldn't wait for my turn to ride the rails.

In my earliest memories I recall sitting on the stoop with my family, at our home in Buena Vista, Ohio. In the twilight of a summer day, I loved watching the lightning bugs blink their love song to each other while sharing the events of the day or listening to one of my parents telling yet another enchanting story. This was a special time for a little fella in the late 1940s in southern Ohio. The evening radio stations had gone quiet after the last of the news and the daily stories. At this time of night it was quiet all around except for an occasional cricket or night bird. It was the peacefulness that only could have been experienced in our rural country village, between the hills bracing the beautiful Ohio River.

It was at this hour of the evening, sitting on the cool stone steps, that I would listen keenly for the sound.

At first it felt as if I were only remembering the sound heard before... Then ever so faintly I could hear it! Coming up river on the Kentucky side, it would whistle as it passed the little Kentucky town of Vanceburg, some three plus miles to the west. At each crossed roads or lane it would sound again, growing louder as it came closer. At last it was fully echoed across the valley... starting with a low tone intensifying to a high pitch, and then dropping off... yet to repeat it twice again... and one more long low moan as it ended.

You could set your watch by the passing of the giant steam engine #790. "Yeppers, 7:53. Right on schedule," as it pulled the George Washington eastbound, barreling towards the mountains of West Virginia, over the Blue Ridge Mountains of the Appalachians and down the Piedmonts, dropping in to the Virginia coastal plains of the James River Valley. Its destination Washington DC.

My mind danced with the visions of the old #790, the powerfully massive black steam locomotive as it hurled eastward, belching steam and smoke, roaring like a huge iron beast consuming mile after mile of track. I envisioned its luxurious car interiors with people onboard, dressed in fineries, or business men in suits, still working on their "butter and eggs" projects. I conjured in my mind, these imagined pictures as the magical sounds filled my head.

This was such a pivotal time in my life.

Living in this tiny Appalachian village, where most of the buildings were constructed in the mid-1800s, life seemed frozen in a time before I was born. This ancient village of around 200 souls existed for, and with, each other. Neighbors were truly neighbors. While other villages and cities had grocery stores, modern schools, pharmacies, police and fire, this stone cutters' village had two small general stores, one place to buy gas, a two room school house and a few volunteers equipped with an old reject fire truck – mainly to keep a fire from spreading.

Buena Vista was in many ways like the mystical village in the movie Brigadoon, consisting of farmers, hunters, and rivermen mostly... where everyone knew each other, everything, both good and bad. This extended family environment made it a wonderful place to grow up.

As I recall, sounds and scents then were of extraordinary importance. The intonation of each tractor-trailer truck, as they transversed our single highway connection to the outside world, would punctuate our day. Old bias tires of those years made a peculiar sound, a high pitched whine of rubber and the highway pavement interacting. As the truck got closer, the distant buzz would steadily grow... then like the crash of a trashcan being dropped, it would roar past in a violent crescendo, then as the Doppler effect reversed into a descending indistinct buzz, it disappeared as it had started.

There was the occasional car horn and the whistle and chugging as the tow boats slowly pushed their barges up or down river.

Man made sounds always got our attention... and there was nothing more engaging and dream-inspiring than the lonesome whistle of the George Washington hurling through field and del on the other side of the river.

I was never privileged to ride or even see up close the smoke and steam belching beast, ever reliably on time. But from memory, the stories told by family members who shared their experiences sitting around a fire at night, told me all I needed to know... I love trains.

As I recall, the folks said that the George Washington was a deluxe Pullman passenger train that ran from Lexington, Kentucky to as far north as New York City beginning in 1932, and was named in honor of our first president. The trip from Lexington to Washington DC took 13 1/2 hours... and you could set your watch by it. In those days it ran on the railroad time.

The George offered all the amenities at that time including sleeper service, diner car with a full menu, the observation car, several Pullman coaches which combined seating and sleeping, and of course private room sleepers.

All of that, of course, was unknown to the little boy sitting on the stone steps. All I knew was the magical sound, its whistle and the deep rumble chugging at a mile a minute on the tracks... happening at the exact same time, seven days a week.

That experience set in motion my lifelong love with trains.

Things have changed greatly since then, some better and some not. My grandmother told me of a trip she once took on a train to Florida. It was posh, luxurious and the service was impeccable. She did mention in passing that there were a lot of men smoking cigars and women smoking cigarettes in the same coach. She wondered aloud, "If all the seating in the lounge car at the end of the train had already been taken." Looking back, that was her code that she would've preferred not to have shared a close space with so many smokers. Keeping in mind that smoking was prevalent in all areas of society during those days. One of the bonuses when riding a train then was that you could open a window to ventilate the car... Of course you would also ventilate in the coal smoke and soot.

Just a note: The air conditioning on trains today will exchange the air approximately every two minutes. I wonder what my grandmother would have said about that.

I have traveled on the same George Washington route, now the Amtrak® Cardinal from the whistle stop in South Portsmouth to the East Coast. There were others including a most memorable trip from Cincinnati to the Great Lakes Naval Training Center for Boot Camp, and returning home three months later. I have enjoyed Amtrak®, on short trips as well as numerous cross-country journeys. Destinations to and from Ohio to Chicago; New York City; Norfolk, Virginia; Charleston, South Carolina; Appleton, Wisconsin; Denver, Colorado; Portland, Oregon; San Francisco and Los Angeles, California... each experience much more the journey than the destination.

I have been privileged to ride in locomotive cabs in the Antioch-Pittsburg railroad yards and even a working day in several others as I could manage. Railroad yards vary from just a few tracks to immense locations that handle dozens of trains on a daily basis, holding thousands of cars for storage or sorting at one place. Total efficiency.

Riding in coach class is always fascinating. Whether it is a new Amtrak® coach or the refurbished short run older Amtrak® cars, the experience is similar. The only difference is space and the quality of the seats. The new Amtrak® cars have seats like recliner chairs in your living room, comfy wide with good lumbar support. The seats are in pairs with an armrest between the two, there is a pair on either side of the aisle. Above are luggage racks where your suitcase and other items can be stored.

The paired seats can be rotated creating a seating for a foursome. This makes it quite easy for you to meet and make new friends.

Riding the rails in Business Class is an affordable, upgrade experience offered on many trains, including extra legroom and complimentary non-alcoholic drinks, reserved seating and are located in a dedicated car or section of the train. You will find private accommodations from two to twelve passengers in Sleeping Cars, that include special amenities on overnight trips. A dedicated attendant provides turndown service, assists with meals, helps with luggage and shares great stories of life on the rails. These private rooms include courtesy lounges at major stations, priority boarding and all meals onboard... a great financial perk.

All across America and throughout the world there are wonderful rail adventures for every taste.

Today there are three cross country rail experiences that I personally have taken. These are great ways to see the United States

The northernmost route on the Empire Builder takes you from Chicago across America's mother waterway, the mighty Mississippi River at St. Paul/Minneapolis. Following the Lewis &

Clark Trail from the grass plains, into the Rocky Mountain's Big Sky country and Glacier National Park to Spokane, you will arrive in the Portland/Seattle area in just under 50 hours.

The California Zephyr cuts across the midsection of America. From your picture window, or the observation car on this historic line, you will be spellbound by the sights that greeted fortune seekers dreaming of striking it rich in the mid 1800's.

For me, this is the most spectacular rail journey available on Amtrak®. From the prairies and grassland covered swaths where countless herds of American Buffalo (bison) once grazed, deep into the Rocky Mountains where tunnels open vistas on the Continental Divide. Golden aspens quake magically in the breeze, as evergreens climb the steep Glenwood Canyon above the Colorado River.

Dropping into Utah's canyon lands among the monoliths where countless western movies have been shot, into the Salt Lake Intermodal Hub, you cross the northern desert of Nevada and climb the Sierra Nevadas. This is the heart of Gold Rush mining area, with ghost towns and old stagecoach stations that were stops on the original railroad. The journey ends over 50 hours later within view of the Golden Gate Bridge.

Epic!

The last of the trilogy train adventures is aboard the Southwest Chief.

My last journey on the Chief was westbound, and I had upgraded to a roomette. Departing the classic ambience of the majestic Great Hall in Chicago's Union Station, I passed through the turnstile onto the Southwest Chief's loading platform... one of fourteen southern stub tracks (ten on the north side). Its massive shed, which once shielded the passenger from the harsh Chi Town weather, are now foundations for massive buildings above.

Following the throng of fellow passengers, I found myself standing beneath the front of a General Electric P40-DC engine, dressed in its Amtrak® livery of red, white and blue. A great black window ten feet above was where the engineer, conductor and driver would control my chariot for the next 2+ days. Mounted within the stripes on the front were two blindingly bright headlights, and centered above just below the word "Amtrak" were two additional lights that would flash and turn like strobes, warning anyone that the train was coming. Below the standard coupler was the modern version of a cow catcher.

The engine stood above me, large, and ready to hurl westward across the western half of our nation.

Walking along the platform I soon found my sleeping car. Moving from the end of the car to the center I climbed a short spiral staircase to the landing on the second level where an attendant escorted me to my roomette. This was to be my home until I arrived in Los Angeles.

Inside were two loveseats facing each other with a table between them. Above was a large picture window fresh and sparkling, ready for my journey. A folded bunk was overhead, which I would not need. On one side of the door was a small closet for a jacket and a couple hangups and on the other was a set of shelving for my necessities. The corridor wall was all glass, with a sliding door, that I would cover later with drapes for privacy.

On the same level was a bathroom with showers and at the top of the spiral stairs was a small refreshment kiosk with fresh coffee, juices, snacks and pastries... All part of the sleeper car service.

I first checked the newsletter on the table which had information about the first day of the journey, the day's schedule and menu. Below on the platform the last of my fellow travelers were boarding, and folks were moving back-and-forth in the corridor settling in. The excitement of heading west was interrupted by a voice on the PA announcing, "Amtrak Southwest Chief from Chicago to Los Angeles will be departing on time," pause, "All aboard!"

The adventure began.

Without warning the train began backing out of the sheds, as each car's connections tightened up with a bump, we moved from darkness into the bright light of a Midwest afternoon. Backing to the switching area, we were directed onto the main line heading into the afternoon sun.

It seemed only moments later that the steward was asking if I would care for coffee or juice, and if I had made an evening's meal choice. He took time to explain that there were two seatings and we had a choice of three entrées. Bringing me coffee and a doughnut I learned that the diner was two cars forward. Soon the suburbs were passing beneath my window, the engineer sounding the horn at every crossing. Platforms filled with people waiting for the local trains to take them home, or waiting for friends and family to be picked up. The scene changed from buildings and homes to vast fields of corn and soybean with co-op silo configurations popping up, and quickly disappearing behind us.

A chime rang over the intercom, "First seating for dinner!" That was me.... I joined others going down the spiral staircase and heading towards the front of the train. Passing through the vestibule between cars, I walked the length of two coach cars filled with passengers either traveling partway, or deciding to take advantage of the recliners and "rough it."

Stepping through the vestibule into the dining car I was greeted by the steward who asked my name and escorted me to my table. If you are traveling single or as a couple you will be asked to share the table with others. My first meal was shared with an elderly couple going to visit their children in Albuquerque, New Mexico. The conversation was great, the food was standard railroad food... generous portions, reasonable quality and served on China. This was going to be a great trip!

This would be the routine for my next two days heading west, with our extraordinary country passing by my window as if it were a 3-D movie... Without the necessary glasses. I saw more history in that 50 hour trip than I had learned in fourteen years of schooling. Nothing like the real thing!

Periodically there would be a fuel stop or change of train crew and this would give us the opportunity to go on the platform for a breath of fresh air, and for "those who had them, Smokem!" One of my most memorable stops on that trip was in Albuquerque where

I said goodbye to my dinner mates and shopped with the Native Americans selling their goods. I bought several things at that stop, and one that I still use today, a money clip with a 1920s Indian head nickel soldered to it.

This trip was much like so many of the other adventures I have had on the rails, some shorter, some a bit longer but all filled with the excitement of seeing our great country, at a leisurely pace... where I didn't have to drive, paying attention to the traffic, or be wedged into a too tight coach seat on an airplane breathing stale air for hours. It is interesting that my total fair for all meals, room with service – and a fantastic view of our country – was less than the first class fare on my favorite airline.

No wonder I love railroads.

Rail travel is changing in America today, with many routes doing away with quality dining cars, substituting re-warmed prepared meals.

Should you decide to explore this mode of travel, please check with your travel agent or Amtrak®. And consider joining one of the excursion trains that will, without a doubt, replicate the train trips of the 30's, 40's or 50's. They're as expensive as a cruise ship... But without the 5,000 passengers vying for the same space aboard, and in the shops in port.

I hope that sharing the story – from a young fellow listening to a train whistle across the river to my adult adventures – will inspire you to consider making your next journey from one place to another, aboard the train.

Not a doubt, riding the rails has been a lifelong addiction for me.

Notes: The time traveling during these experiences will vary depending on weather and rail traffic conditions. (Amtrak® shares the rails with commercial freight trains.)

Pullman perfected the railcar and became so successful that the term "Pullman" generally described the car, even if a particular one wasn't built by the company. Early car designs offered some type of berth arrangement whereby the seats could be laid out into a bed.

Rolf Andersson and Inga Maj Nilsson
Dalsland, Sweden

- 18 -

The Train that Shouldn't Have Become a Ferry

Inga Maj and I were on the train to Helsingborg, Sweden, going to visit some cousins of hers. They had plans for me to have a day visit in Copenhagen and I was excited at the prospect. It was a city I'd always longed to see and now was the time!

Inga Maj and I had set out from the small town of Dals-Ed early that morning and had enjoyed a great train trip. The scenery was always spectacular and the conversation lively, planning what I might have time to see in the city during our brief overnight stay.

The train pulled into Helsingborg, and it was time to disembark and meet cousins Margareta and Per at the station. Inga Maj saw no platform near our car and assumed we were simply waiting to pull into the station. So we waited in our seats.

During the journey, she had explained to me that the train would continue to the Danish side of the Sound after we disembarked in Helsingborg. It would pull directly onto the ferry and float across the water to Denmark. I was astounded!

And, at eighteen, I was full of questions. "You mean, the passengers just sit in the train while it floats on a ferry across the water??"

Yes, Virginia, there is a train that becomes a ferry.

As we sat there waiting for the train to completely pull into the station, we heard all the doors lock. Inga Maj looked panicked. I didn't understand what was happening. "Where are we heading now?"

"On the way towards Denmark!" Inga Maj did her best to calm herself and continue to patiently address all my excited questions.

So I would get to experience the train-ferry after all! How exciting!

After the train pulled onto the ferry, the doors unlocked and Inga Maj excitedly jumped up and scurried for the closest door, me following as best I could. We managed to get off the train and into the ferry itself.

It was not well lit at all. Everyone else had already left the train to go topside. We looked left, then right, then left again. Signage was confusing. And so I followed quickly after Inga Maj as she looked for the way out. We went this way, and that way, and it began to feel as if we were in some sort of fun house, and it was quickly losing its "fun-ness!"

So we hurried even faster along the rail track and finally found a stairway. Just as we broke into daylight, huffing and puffing, Inga Maj looked out past the rail of the ferry deck and bleated, "Oh! Oh no!! We're heading to Helsingør!"

Sure enough, we were headed across the five mile stretch of Øresund between Sweden and Denmark. We'd missed our disembarkation entirely.

Margareta and Per were likely still at the station in Sweden. Hopefully, they would wait for us to return from our unplanned trek to Denmark! There were no cell phones at that time. No way to let them know what had happened.

I can only imagine what they must have thought as they watched the train vanish into the bowels of the ferry and never saw us on the platform or in the station!

So! Now what?

And that's exactly what I asked Inga Maj. "What do we do now?"

Truth be told, there was *nothing* we could do. Like it or not we were along for the ride. And that is pretty much what she told me.

It was a beautiful sunny day, and we might as well just take in the scenery on our round trip voyage across the sound to Helsingør, Denmark and back to Sweden.

We stayed up on deck, at the rail, wind in our hair, just watching the Sound go by as Sweden faded and Denmark grew larger.

As we got closer, Kronborg Castle came into view on the opposite shore. Inga Maj became very excited, telling me what it was and explaining the connection to Shakespeare's Hamlet.

Standing next to us on the deck was a couple who became interested, also, in what Inga Maj was saying. The only catch was… they didn't speak English. Inga Maj is multi-lingual and so tried out other ways to communicate with them.

Swedish? No.

German? No.

And at that point, Inga Maj was out of options.

So she did what only Inga Maj could do. She started flailing her arms, pointing, and yelling wildly, "Hamlet! Hamlet's Castle! 'To beeeee or not to beeeee…' Shakespeare! Hamlet's Castle!"

She repeated it many times, they smiled and nodded vehemently as if they understood. To this day, I'm still not sure whether they truly got it or whether she scared the bejeebers out of them and they smiled and nodded like any kind soul would do with a crazy ranting person.

Either way she appeared satisfied that she'd passed along the knowledge as a good tour guide would. When we reached Denmark, we watched people disembark, more people joined us, and before we knew it, we were on our way back to Sweden once again.

We made sure we were right where we needed to be to disembark the ferry this time.

Her cousins were indeed there to meet us, and we told them the hilarious tale on the ride to their home. We all got a good belly laugh.

To this day, 35 years later, I still tell the story, and laugh every bit as hard as I did that day. It is a favorite in Inga Maj's circle as well. They call it the Train Ferry Story.

Inga Maj always had a way of making the best of a less than perfect situation. She made it fun. Even when it looked as if she was truly losing it, she still managed to find the humor in most things. She didn't waste a single moment of fretting overly about things she couldn't change.

I learned a lot from her, particularly that it was ok to laugh like a mad person when life was really going off the rails, per se. (Pun absolutely intended!) Things would most always work themselves out if you let some time pass. In this instance, it was about 45 minutes to make the round trip! And things surely did work out just fine.

So often in life things do not go quite how we planned or expected. The road goes left instead of right, down instead of up. People we thought would always be there are suddenly gone, for any number of reasons. And all the planning we put our heart and soul into must be rethought because some power out of our control deemed things to happen differently.

Nothing in life is guaranteed. Actually, the only thing we are guaranteed is that we don't (can't!) know what will happen, nor when, nor with whom... and that we are not immortal. The old adage about death and taxes. We must rely on not being able to rely.

Challenging at best, devastating at worst.

Don't let it devastate you. If you truly cannot change it, make the best of it however you can. If you can't manage that, then try to wait it out... for the pain to dull, for a new idea to arrive, for peace to come into your soul once again.

No one knows what tomorrow will bring. I, for one, don't want to know. Whatever it is, roll with it. Do your best to develop a sense of humor about the things that simply will not matter next week, or five years from now. Recognize them, accept them, and remember Inga Maj... there is laughter in there somewhere.

- 19 -
The Comet Mound, Place of My Traditions

"I am Shawnee! I am a warrior! My forefathers were warriors. From them I took my birth into this world. From my tribe I take nothing. I am the master of my own destiny!" - Shawnee War Chief Tecumseh.

I am Shawnee! More precisely, I am of the Panji Seepe Naube... the People of the Blue Creek Way. Before the People of the South Wind, the Shawnee, came into our lands to make a confederacy with my people, we were always and forever the People of the Earth.

This we believe.

We are taught that Grandmother Kitch Tula, the Earth, is the "great preparer of all things." She takes the seed from Grandfather Sky and plants them within her flesh to be nurtured and to grow us into Two-Leggeds. She also takes the seed of every living thing and makes them likewise alive.

With respect, and to honor our Grandmother of All Life, our ancestors made great monuments to all the creatures she birthed, by mounding her flesh into effigy likenesses. Because our Grandmother Earth gave us life, we are forever the People of the Earth.

This we believe.

I am a warrior as were all my ancestors. We have always been warriors. Not that fighting is our way of life, but that we must be ever strong to ensure, and obey, the principle decree of our faith... "Never let the people die." It means to always create new generations and to never allow the sacred teachings to be forgotten. To be a warrior was to be strong no matter the adversity, the danger, no matter what life would present... we were given the Way.

This we believe

My Panji Seepe Naube ancestors were taught this ancient Path... the Mide' Way... the law passed down from our elders that requires us to discover and understand the meaning and the practices of the levels of the Sky, and the levels of the Earth.

I am a Midewiwan, one who walks the Path of the Mide' Way.

I was taught this ancestral spiritual path one on one, on back steps, on the banks of the Spaylaywitheepi, the Ohio River, and in the sacred Place of the Comet – mistakenly referred to by strangers as the Serpent Mound. It is here that my uncle and aunt, as is the proper way, taught me all things sacred. He taught me why, and how, everything we do, and know, relates to each of the levels of the Sky, and she taught me of the mysticism and magic that is found when we learn of each level of the Earth.

Much of this teaching was done sitting on the rocks at the base of the cliff below the effigy that is the Comet Mound. It is here that I first drank from the aquifer that our ancestors believe to be Water of the Ancestors Spirits. From that water everything flows within and around us.

This I believe.

It is not proper to share with you the intrinsic learnings of the Levels, but that you, the descendants from foreign lands, and other First Peoples not of our ancestors' seed, might find meaning and enlightenment in this Sacred Place. The secrets passed down from mouth to ear belong only to the few who descend from our ancestors. You may believe that you are descended, but if you truly are, we will know.

The difference is everything. This we believe.

My aunt once told me that she was particularly pleased when families would come to this sacred place, to have picnics and enjoy each other's company. She had been taught that this was where one could find happiness and contentment.

Interestingly though, my uncle reminded me that this was where we learned to separate Earth People from Grandfather Sky's seed People who made the mound from Tula's flesh, and empowered its magic.

I came to know that both were right. Like so many of the most powerful and sacred places around the world – the Earth below, and the Sky above – these sacred places are empowering and comforting.

Some may believe that keeping our spiritual path private, and not sharing it with non-descended people, is selfish or wrong. In truth, our particular faith is based on our connectedness to our unique ancestors. If this lack of sharing concerns you, I only offer that you study the path of your own ancestors, and learn of their ways, their original beliefs and how they kept them... and why.

If you so choose, you will learn that this is your history, of your people and your rightful path to enlightenment. There is no right, nor wrong choice, for we are all walking from the Outer Circle to the Center where our Creator resides.

May your path be of greatness for you, that fulfills your needs, and gives you hope for that eternity that we all seek.

Always, walk towards the center, and always... Walk in Balance.

This I believe.

The Aquifer at Brush Creek
Comet Mound, Adams County, Peebles, OH

"Baba"
Helen Cisar Rericha

- 20 -
Baba's Great Wisdom

Baba was a tiny little bundle of love, patience, and fierce resilience. She laughed easily, had the kindest eyes I've ever seen, and never let life get her down. Sure, she'd known heartache, plenty of it... and once in a while, things got her mad. But never in her almost 93 years did she ever consider giving up, or not accepting whatever life dealt her.

I had the honor of being in her life for almost two decades and I sure did learn a lot. I actually "met" her on a phone call with my future husband Bryan, long before we even considered ourselves as "dating." Bryan put her on the line, asking me to wish her greetings on her 76th birthday. She was a delight... happy, fun-loving, and always eager to be kind to someone Bryan cared for.

She adored him. She was the epitome of a doting grandma to him. His mother's mother, she spent part of her time living in Bryan's parents' home and the adoration was mutual between her and her grandson.

Baba loved to cook. And it just so happened that she cooked exactly like my own grandma used to – they were of the same culture, Bohemian (Czechoslovakian). Every day when Bryan came home from university classes, she would leave a "love offering" on the end of the kitchen counter for him. Some small snack to tide him over until dinner was ready. Even today, he still browses the kitchen counter in our own home, looking for snacking tidbits during dinner prep. I always think of her when he does.

Baba never wore a pair of slacks (that I ever saw anyway). She wore hose – literally hose with garters – a skirt, blouse, and usually a cardigan type sweater. And always "sensible" shoes. Her version of dressing down were cotton "house dresses" that she would wear when doing housework. Usually sleeveless, plaid or striped, and pockets. They always had to have pockets for Baba's miscellaneous necessities. When she was cooking, she always wore an apron over her clothes, no matter whether it was her street clothes or her "house dresses."

Despite her size, Baba was a sturdy and determined little woman. By the time I met her, she was in her mid-70s and still full of energy. She had her share of aches and pains by then, but that never stopped her from keeping herself busy. Baba wasn't an idle woman. She was a whirling dervish at times but she always acknowledged, with grace, when enough was enough for her, and she would stop, take a break, and catch her wind. When the second wind came, she was up and at it again.

She was raised on a farm in central Ohio, in a coal mining community. Her life was rural, and hardworking, and simple. Baba and her six siblings were first born Americans to Bohemian (Czechoslovakian) parents. Taught responsibility and industriousness from a young age, she carried those principals through her entire life.

It always amazed me how much she could get done in fits and starts. She would take on, what appeared to be, large and energetic projects for such a frail looking little woman. But by the end of the day, everything was done, cleaned up, and Baba was ready to help make dinner.

On warm sunny days, when staying with Bryan's parents, she would announce she was going out to clean up the yard for the burn barrel. They didn't have garbage pickup in their rural area at that time so they burned household trash. Baba loved to burn. She would go out into the expanse of the backyard and begin picking up twigs and sticks. It gave her a great excuse to get some walking in and she would come back to the barrel and dump in what she'd found. Now and then she'd find a seat and just watch the world go by, then she'd be up again scrounging for more "fuel." Near the end, you'd see her coming back dragging branches as long as she was tall. Everything went into the barrel, along with the day's trash, and then you'd see bright orange flame and Baba out there tending over it like a stew pot. Poking, pushing, prodding... until it was all burned down.

We have a phrase in our household, "Pull a Baba on it." It means doing something which seems insurmountable, one bite at a time. Don't get overwhelmed, just start and do one step at a time until it is done.

The mindset of taking things one step at a time is only one of so many things I learned from Baba. She was a formative character not only in Bryan's life, but in my own as well. Some other lessons we both learned from her…

1. **Don't hold grudges.** And she didn't. She didn't forget… but she didn't waste energy on prolonged anger and bitterness. It happened, it's over, learn to be wary for next time if you must, but move on. Don't dwell on it.

2. **Love your family with the deepest devotion.** Baba showed love every minute of every day to the ones she held most dear. When she would visit Bryan and me, sometimes he would lay with his head on her lap and she would stroke his mop of dark hair and tell him how much she loved him. I have a photo of them this way that is priceless. It is the perfect capture of how deeply and tenderly she loved.

3. **Don't meddle.** She made a point of staying out of the affairs of others. Baba let other people work out their own issues. She was always there to listen, and to state her opinion if asked, but she did not push those opinions on anyone else. She was incredibly gracious in that way.

4. **Accept what life brings with grace and a certain determination.** Baba lived almost 93 years and I rarely saw her truly "upset" about anything. Things that would send most of us into fits of frustration didn't even faze her. She simply accepted what could not be changed and determined to find how best to live with it.

5. **Choose to laugh and have a good time.** She always had a laugh right near the surface, ready to burst out in a contagious way. She didn't take much of anything too seriously and

always had a plan for when to put her feet up – literally! – and have a cold beer. She never let life get her down.

I wish everyone could have a Baba in their life. Someone who has lived a lot of life and refuses to be bitter about the challenging parts, only choosing to put energy into remembering the best parts. Someone who loves with no judgment or expectation. Someone who teaches through her actions, showing graciously how to take life one step at a time, never succumbing to overwhelm or frustration.

It's a lesson beyond value. She is in our family stories often, and they are always told with a smile and laughter. That is what she brought to us... and left with us.

Next time you face a challenge, "pull a Baba on it" and carry on as if it wasn't even a speed bump in your life.

- 21 -
Mushroom Double Cheese Pizza & Tanqueray

A long time ago I lived with someone who worked the night shift. It was a very different way of living and a schedule I was completely and utterly unfamiliar with.

At that time in my life, I *really* didn't like to be alone. I had not yet cultivated the ability to just "be with one's self." Quite frankly, it scared me. I'd never slept in an empty home before... someone had always been, at maximum, within shouting distance at night. And I'd never had to entertain myself during the evenings.

I won't say I was young but I was most definitely immature about this type of experience. I had no clue how to go about being with myself evening after evening, night after night.

As they say, practice makes perfect – and I had lots of practice during those few years. Eventually I got over my fear and learned that I could be pretty good company for myself.

I read a lot, even more than usual. And I had plenty of time to catch up with my sister – we *never* ran out of things to talk about – as well as my mom, and a cousin's wife, with whom I was really close. I remember those "girl" conversations with deep nostalgia. They were great relationship builders.

At that time I was a graphic designer and learning to be a web developer. I sometimes worked into the evening... because I could, no responsibility to cook or interact. That part allowed me to keep going on a project if I was on a creative roll, and even learn new skills.

Looking back on it, I got a lot done during those years. Most importantly, though, I grew up a lot. I learned it was ok to be with myself, and just myself. I didn't die of loneliness, I didn't waste away from fright.

It sounds odd to many people who really like to be alone. The person I lived with at the time was one of those and could never understand my angst.

But being alone is a real fear, for many people, and I was one of them. And, if I'm honest, as I always am with you dear reader, I still can't say it's one of my favorite things. I have just learned to make the best of it on those occasions when I find myself alone in the house outside of work hours.

It's obviously another face of the separation anxiety that has plagued me my entire life. Dad died before I was born, and so I was always terrified I would lose someone else close to me. I was six years old and seeing a child psychologist because my mother couldn't take me to school... I'd have a meltdown every time when she would walk away from me and leave me there. But that's a story covered elsewhere in this book (*Mrs. Tinker Taught Me to Trust*).

The scars still remain and raise their ugly head in new and interesting and wholly unpleasant ways. But! As I've already said, I learned. I learned to entertain myself and that, while being alone wasn't preferable to me, I could cope.

One way I coped, was to treat myself once a month or so. My favorite treat was ordering a pizza just for myself. I'd never ever dreamed of doing such a thing! Pizza was for family, for friends, for a *group* of people. Not just little ol' me. I thought myself so daring at the time!

My first outing was strange and exciting. I love cheese. And I love mushrooms. So... I called up the local pizza joint and ordered a small double cheese and mushroom only pizza! Never had I had the luxury of getting *just and only* what *I* wanted. No compromising. It was just for me. I was amazed and filled with wonder at the daring concept.

Once I break through a fear, I quickly adapt and find the next daring thing I can do. And so the next time, on my way to the pizza joint, I dared to walk into the liquor store – in Ohio they are state run and were stand-alone establishments at that time (e.g., one's sole purpose for being in that store was to *buy liquor*). Now *this* was damn near shameless and bold. Me. Alone. Going to buy booze. Just. For. Me. To go with my.... you got it... double cheese and mushroom only pizza.

I love gin and tonics, and so my treat would be to buy the smallest bottle of Tanqueray they had. I usually had to ask for the one behind the counter because those are too small for them to put out on the shelves. I'd buy some tonic water and a lime if they had it and off I would go to claim my little pizza.

Those evenings were, in a lot of ways, magical to me. I'd watch a "chick flick" in my jammies, eat my pizza, and have a cocktail or two. Who knew it could be like this? It became a way to nurture myself, and reward myself for weeks of hard work and accomplishments.

I learned I could be alone, with myself, and actually enjoy it. I learned I could reward myself and that I didn't necessarily need for someone else to do it.

Fears are meant to be vanquished. It's a rite of passage.

And everyone deserves to experience it. To use a pitifully overused word... It's totally empowering. And a great ego boost.

You are capable of things you cannot even fathom right now. You may not know it, but I do. Whatever your story, your background, you can do wondrous and amazing things. Some of them may seem simple to others, and some may seem heroic. Either way, if they are a way for you to conquer and move forward, that is all that matters.

What are your fears? Pick the worst one. Decide how you can get on the other side of it, so to speak. Do it with deliberate action and planning. Set yourself up for success and then go get 'em.

I believe in you. So should you.

- 22 -
LADIES OF SAIGON

This is a story of hard truths, apolitical observations, and undeniable results.

After a year and a half in college, I decided to join the military. Not because college life was boring or dissatisfying, but because I could not convince my parents to not help me with the tuition. I was a music major at the University of Dayton and didn't need their help. A college kid who didn't need help with tuition? In my case, no. I was a professional member of the American Federation of Musicians and was working regularly. Playing gigs in night clubs and for special occasions, I was making much more than I needed for tuition, board and keep. I was living the high life!

But I couldn't convince my mom and dad that I didn't need their hard earned $500 every semester. Fact was, they were also saving money to help my younger siblings.

Mom and pop felt obligated to help us with our financial needs. My family descended from a mix of Scots-Irish, Jewish and Native Americans, making us a strong willed people.

We were at loggerheads... The immovable against inertia.

Knowing that I couldn't win I decided to leave college for a while, and join the Marines. My sister was a Marine, and had married a decorated Korean War Marine. Additionally, my cousin George, "Puddenhead," was a Marine who served in the South Pacific Theater during World War II. Add to the mix my uncle who was an Essex Scottish Black Watch Canadian commando during the European conflict of World War II.

I was surrounded by bad ass warriors.

Putting on my best suit I went to the recruiting station in downtown Dayton. I boldly walked up to the Marine sergeant at the desk and said, "I want to be a Marine!" He looked me up-and-down, leaning back in his chair said,"The Marines don't take fat boys!"

I was gobsmacked. "Fat boy?" My heart sank into my shoes, I was devastated.

My chin was firmly planted on my chest with the rejection. Stumbling towards the door, I heard a soft voice say, "Come here son!" It was the Navy recruiter, a Chief Boatswain Mate... Just like my dad. As they say the rest was history.

I spent the next three months at Great Lakes Naval Training Center, and upon graduation, I deployed to my new duty station – MINPAC-MINRON 11, MINDIV 116 – in Navy "code" that meant I was to be a "deck ape" in Long Beach, California.

Impossible! My Chief in Boot Camp promised I was going to band school on the East Coast. But... There's a saying in the military, SNAFU, situation normal, all f'ed up!

I was assigned to a very small boat, the MSB (Mine Sweep Boat) 54 as an able-bodied seaman, whose basic job was to paint, chip paint, sand and repaint anything that didn't move. That was a far cry from being a talented musician in a Navy Band.

The education that I was receiving as a sailor was quite different from being a college kid. Gone were the days of music classes and band practice, casually going from one class to another and having a really great time on campus. All that frivolity had been replaced with organization, responsibility and discipline. Talk about growing up fast. I was now assigned to a modified wooden "fishing trawler" boat that was expendable. In combat we were the front line of the Navy along the shore, finding underwater mines, bombs set to destroy ships of war... and to dispose of them. Life instantly became heartbeat serious, and very dangerous.

Between operations, the work in port was the tedious and boring work of maintenance. Not very exciting, I looked for opportunities for diversion. I learned quickly that if I volunteered for special assignments as they came available, I would spend less time as a "deck ape."

One assignment I took was to work as a cartographer, plotting for our unit's sweeping exercises while at sea. I also volunteered for time at the firing range, and for survival training as they came available.

All this was preparatory to my next assignment... a special insertion into Vietnam to chart potential pier sites for the yet-to-be-built PCF Swift Boats. I deployed several times to Vietnam, charting various aspects of the Mekong River Delta. Did I mention that this was very exciting... And damn dangerous!

It was on one of these assignments that I was given a day off for R&R, Rest and Relaxation. I took the opportunity to go to Saigon just to see what that big city was all about.

For an Appalachian country boy, it was beyond anything I could imagine. It was a tropical paradise with new buildings interspersed amongst an ancient culture.

I recall the taxi dropping me off on a broad boulevard along the riverfront. Everywhere was the intoxicating floral aromas of frangipani and yellow mimosa intermingled with pungent sweet fragrances of lotus flowers and the orchid tree. Some more familiar scents were sweet peas and morning glories. These and other exotic flowers blended with garlic and soy – it was indescribably oriental. Add the incessant ringing of bicycle bells and motor scooters whizzing by... simply intoxicating!

I entirely forgot about the constant danger on the river and the war that was around us. I could finally relax in the moment and enjoy this day. This truly was R&R, a restful and relaxing time.

As I was sitting on a concrete bench, just taking this all in and relaxing, I was approached by three elderly Vietnamese ladies, dressed in traditional black. As they approached I could see one had a muskmelon in her hands. I rose and bowed my head in respect to the elders. "Namaste."

The ladies formed a semi circle in front of me, and the woman with the melon deftly pulled a folding farmer's knife from under her clothing. It was a basic handmade knife, scales made of hardwood, a single pivot bolt and a hand forged machete sized blade. It was a functional tool of farmers, not a weapon.

Opening the big knife she cut the melon into four pieces. She handed a piece of the melon to each of us. Using our fingers we scraped away the seeds and began to eat. It was one of the sweetest melons I have ever tasted. Fully ripe, it was a perfect repast on a steamy hot Southeast Asian day.

As we sat on the bench, enjoying the melon, what small talk we attempted was of little success. They spoke only Vietnamese, and a bit of French, and I spoke only English, and a few words of French. The majority of the conversation consisted of hand signs and smiles... and appropriate head nods. Soon the melon was gone. The conversation going nowhere, we rose and smiled warmly at each other.

Then it happened.

The lady who presented the melon, stepped close to me and, with tears in her eyes, gently placed her hand on my chest. Softly she said, "You." Then placing her hand on her chest said, "Make me... free!"

I instantly understood.

The elders of South Vietnam were placing their entire faith in the United States and our powerful military to free them from the relentless communism of North Vietnam's dictator Ho Chi Minh.

They were both hopeful and fearful.

Their fear was well-founded and their hope destroyed. We betrayed them on both accounts. We promised them protection and military aid to defeat their enemy to the north, and we sucked from them the very wind of freedom and hope as we abandoned them in our bug-out!

The incessant war protest mobs, without regard to the unintended consequences... created one. The inevitable was obvious to many Vietnamese. These brave boat people found ways to escape the onslaught that was to come. I have met many of these honorable refugees throughout my life, all are so thankful have become United States citizens.

Those were the lucky few.

After our abandonment of the people of Vietnam, the North Vietnamese and Chinese Communists swept through the country in a horrific purge. Between them and their dictator Cambodian ally, Pol Pot, millions of Southeast Asians were murdered.

We must never forgive nor forget that America betrayed a trust. There are no words!

As a veteran I am ashamed to my core.

The lesson we must learn is plain. We must never allow ourselves to be swayed against our core values by loud voices that demand change without first understanding the unintended consequences of complying with their demands.

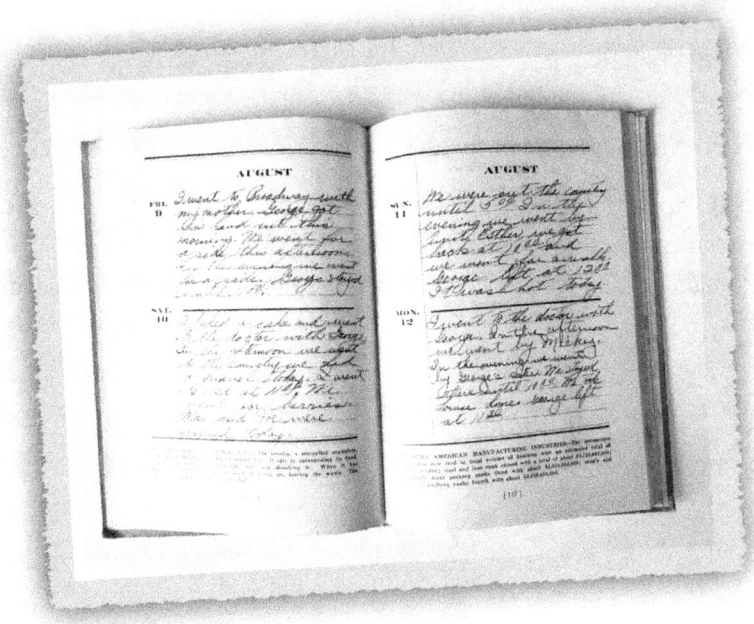

Grandma Violet's
Daily Journal 1929

- 23 -

Grandma Violet's Daily Journal

"The idea is to find some bit of holiness in everything – food, sex, earning and spending money, having children, conversations with friends. Everything can be seen as a miracle, as part of God's plan. When we can truly see this, we nourish our souls." - Rabbi Harold S. Kushner

Grandma Violet kept a diary the entire year of 1929. She was dating my future Grandpa George at the time. She used a "Ready Reference Diary – The Book of 1000 Facts" from The May Co of Cleveland, Ohio.

On the very first page she has handwritten her name, Violet Makovec. On the next page she has a short list of names, addresses, and phone numbers (in the old notation of letters and numbers both).

All the interior pages contained nine lines for entries on each of two days, and at the bottom was a nifty little factoid, or helpful hint – hence the subtitle "The Book of 1000 Facts." A bit of an overstatement perhaps for a book with only 183 pages for days of the year. But..! It also has several helpful pages in the back for everything from tips from "How to Live Long" and dieting advice to cash account pages for savings and tips on how to bid at bridge. There are population numbers for cities over 25,000, poison antidotes, and information on the growth of certain tree species. The very last pages are reserved for more personal records, dates, and details.

For such a small little book, it sure packed a punch of value.

For me, however, having discovered it in the 2010s, the value runs far deeper than the tidbits it provided for my 19/20 year old grandmother in 1929.

I have read every page of it, several times over. It is a fascinating glimpse into the everyday life of a lower middle class Eastern European girl and her family, in Cleveland, Ohio just before and after (the original and terrible) "Black Friday."

In few words, but through repetition of themes, she tells me about her relationship with her parents, and her fiancé, my grandfather.

Times were surely "different" then. Downtown Cleveland was a bustling and vibrant place, and our little neighborhood had a Broadway Avenue that was equally vibrant with commerce, movie theaters, gathering spots, and dance halls.

Through my grandmother's eyes, I see a life full of the discovery of "holiness in everything." Not the religious sort – although she *was* raised in the Roman Catholic church – but more of the secular bit. The kind of holiness referred to in Rabbi Kushner's quote above. The mundane, if you will.

One thing she loved to do and did often was taking rides to "the country." Her family had a farm outside the city to which they escaped regularly. It was a quiet place to spend time, have a picnic, enjoy the drive there and back, and enjoy the fresh air.

More often than not the rides happened as a Sunday family outing. Her entries of these trips begin in April and continue into October. It must have been a place where they really had fun and could relax.

During the year of 1929, my grandmother spent time with friends, shopping, baking, "visiting." There were visits to her own "gramma," other family members, and her friends. Although she never goes into detail about them, visiting was a big part of her life. She placed value in keeping connected with her friends and family through face to face interactions.

In 1929, what else was there? Telephones were mostly party lines that were shared by several households, and its very nature meant little to no privacy assurance during conversations. Visiting in person was the only way to have meaningful conversations between neighbors and friends.

Cleaning and laundry were mentioned frequently also. It was simply a part of her life that she reported in a matter of fact way. No opinions, just fact. "We washed today." "We started our house cleaning today." "We finished our house cleaning today." "Ironed today." Household chores were done before anything else. They are always the first mentioned in the day's entry.

One thing I learned growing up in this Eastern European culture, work ethic was foremost in everyone's mind. Whether working at home chores, or working for an employer, it was your duty and responsibility to hold good work habits above any personal enjoyment. Work first, play later. That was the rule of life.

She and my future grandfather also spent a lot of evenings at a place called the Olympia. The Olympia was a movie theater back in a time when "movies" were very new. In fact, it was in the year of 1929 that the real shift from silent film to "talkies" happened. That had to be a very exciting time for movie theater goers such as my grandparents.

Page after page, my grandmother tells the story of her year, both mundane and exciting. Illness and health. Happy times and times that could have been better. It is a peek into a life I never knew she led. Stories she didn't tell. I'm grateful to have found it and it is now a cherished piece of our family history.

Grandma Violet knew how to find the bits of holiness in her everyday life. Whether washing clothes or taking in a new movie on a date with my grandfather, she found it important to mention even the small parts of her days. Parts we would nowadays find inconsequential to mention.

But, you see, it really was a "simpler time" in 1929. There were no cacophony of multi media constantly vying for her attention. She never even mentioned listening to a radio... not once, in the whole year of entries. It was quiet, and focused on relationships with others – friends, family, neighbors – not on consuming information from all around the globe every second of every day.

She had time to visit with her friends. She had time to go for a ride out to the country on a beautiful summer day. And she also had time to ensure her chores were done when they were expected to be done.

And in all of it, she found her rhythm of life. One she enjoyed. And for one year, she recorded it.

What would your life be like if you slowed down? Could you slow down? Would you like to try? For a day, for a week? Disconnect.

Find the holy bits in your life. They are all around you. Take some time to appreciate them like Grandma Violet did. It's a worthy exercise.

- 24 -
Pop Broke His Back

The first sign that there was a problem was a horn beeping, our car's horn. It was familiar, but the urgency wasn't. It was mid week and Pop had driven up to northern Ohio last Sunday, where he was working.

Strange..?

This story I'm about to tell you took place in the village of Buena Vista in Scioto County, Ohio. It was around 1950 and my folks had moved back from central Ohio, to their roots in the place of their Shawnee ancestors and family.

By way of backstory... In 1941, America finally entered World War II. My dad who had previously served in WWI, enlisted in the Navy. He was designated a Seabee (Construction Battalion) because of his previous construction skills.

Dad's brother George had immigrated to Canada in 1939 to join the Essex Scottish Black Watch. to defend our ancestral Scotland which was under invasion. As generations of our warriors before, he was a fierce fighter and served the British Kingdom in that role.

He had moved his family to Fairfield, Ohio (now Fairborn) before deploying to Canada. Upon dad's enlistment in 1941, my family had moved there also, to be near George's family.

After the war, my family moved back to southern Ohio where they were raised, and to be with their parents and near kinfolk. Family has always been important and this was the place to be.

Our families had lived along the Ohio River since it was settled, and before. It was there that our Scots-Irish and Jewish kin met our Native American side... who themselves had lived in this area for millennium upon millennium. These First People were the Panji Seepe (Blue Creek People), a clan of Algonquian speaking

Shawandasse Indians. They had intermarried with the first settlers, the Barber and Waters families, and God only knows what other lines.

We were, and still are, old souls in an older land.

Mom and dad had moved into a little village about a stone's throw from both sets of parents, called Buena Vista. They bought a derelict old two-story frame house with a shed roof add-on, that had been built around 1850. The place had no running water nor plumbing. We had a hand dug cistern out back, and beyond the garden at the end of the lot, was the outhouse. There was a barn and nothing much more. Primitive is an understatement.

Now Pop was real handy, as were most men in his era. Soon he had plumbed a hand pump into the summer kitchen from the cistern. Running water... of a sort, it was indoor plumbing at least. Having worked in the REA, bringing electricity for the first time in wide swaths of the region, he soon had wired the house for electricity.

That meant there was one light in the ceiling in the front room, one in the middle room, one in the shed add-on and one in the summer kitchen. Four lightbulbs in four rooms, with the drop extension to plug-in appliances. Resembling an octopus floating beneath the ceiling, it was a sight to behold. The only addition to modern times was a party line, hand cranked wall phone in the dining room. We were now modern... Living big!

Back to my original story...

The incessant horn beeping outside continued, rousing us from the house and bringing the neighbors onto their front porches. Mom was the first out of the door followed by all the young'ns, like chicks following a hen. The excitement and clamor turned instantly to dread and fear.

Pop was hurt!

From the stoop, we could see dad slumped on the steering wheel of the old Chevy. Sweat was pouring off him. Pop looked real bad.

Mom ran around to the driver side, just as a neighbor from across the street came running. They helped dad to his feet, through the wrought iron gate, up the time worn stone steps and into the house.

I had never seen my dad cry, but I believe he was near to that point... with pain.

It wasn't all that hot that day but his shirt and pants were soaked. We helped him into the middle room which served as our dining room and kitchen. Pop had just driven near five hours to get home, and he collapsed onto a dining chair. My brother and I unlaced his boots as Mom helped him take off his work shirt.

Her mouth dropped open as she looked at her husband's chest area. She shot ramrod straight and started to weep. "Jim, are you all right?" she asked, My dad answered with an emotionless exhaustion, factly stated, "Not really Nell, my back's broke."

The smell of fresh plaster filled the house like wet river bottom mud after a flood. Like a barrel around pop's midsection, his body cast went from his armpits to just above his hip bones. It was white and you could see the wide strips of cloth that the plaster bonded to. It looked like a mummy wrap. It was surreal.

These were strong country folk who lived through World War I, the Great Depression and World War II, but this was a time that tried their mettle.

Mom set about gently cleaning him up, and getting him into a pair of pajamas. We helped him slowly move into the living room, and get seated in the Amen chair. There he could see out the corner window. The only medicine he had was a bottle of aspirin and a jug of moonshine. Between the two he was able to endure the pain... barely.

I don't remember much about the story of the accident, but here are the pieces I put together. Dad was a Journeyman Ironworker. He would "boom out," meaning he was working away from home during the week, but was home most weekends.

He had been in a "raising gang," moving about the midwest erecting the steel framework of buildings, large and small. It paid good money and work was sparse in the Appalachian foothills of southern Ohio.

The gang had finished erecting the main columns and crossbeams, making the skeleton plumb and strong. That day they had been filling in the smaller floor joists and miscellaneous steel... when it happened.

One of the hundred pound plus "junior beams" the crane was swinging in, slipped from the wire cable "choker," and fell... striking him in the mid lumbar region. Vertebrae fractured. His back was broken. The crew rushed him to the hospital, in the back seat of our car, for there wasn't ambulance service in the area.

Shot up with pain killer, the doctors stabilized the injury, fit a body sock around his midsection and wrapped his torso with strips of plaster soaked cloth. Soon the cast was set.

The next morning Pop drove himself home. It had to be a terribly painful hours long trip.

This was bad. We had no insurance and the hospital only gave him a few pain pills, "To hold him over until he got home."

The next couple of weeks were quiet around the house, for dad needed the rest. He lived on the aspirin and country squeezin's... moonshine! It deadened the pain and allowed healing to start. Pop was slow moving around the house. He listened to the radio when he could get a signal, and spent much of the time reading whatever he could get his hands on, and every evening the Good Book.

Things slowly improved.

One morning the phone rang. Mom answered, and said, "Jim, it's for you." Dad was on the phone for a few minutes, hung the receiver on the hook and turned to mom. He took her by the hand and they walked into the bedroom. We could hear them whispering. Once I heard mom say, "But honey, you're not ready... you can't!"

The call was from his boss saying that he couldn't hold his job any longer. Either dad had to come back to work or he'd be fired.

(Authors note... while editing this chapter I became overwhelmed with emotion. I was a little eight-year-old boy sitting on a chair in our dining room listening to my mom and dad. The pain of it all swelled up as if it were happening right at this moment, all over again. I share this because, like you, there are memories that cannot fade and that live forever within us. My tears are dry and I continue.)

This was probably when I first realized that we were kinda poor. Later I learned that although mom was a school teacher, and that dad had steady work, our total income for that year was less than $1200. The average family income in 1950 was $3,300. Even in those times that was a hard scrabble. My brother and I did a bit of hunting and fishing and my sisters gardened with mom. My dad's parents had a small restaurant and helped out whenever they could. We never went without a meal, and always offered visitors to sit down and have a bite.

Truth is dad had a family to feed, so he had to go back to work.

I remember well the morning when dad called my older brother into the dining room and handed him a hacksaw blade. "Be careful son," he said, "Now start here under my arm and cut this damn thing off of me." Soon the cast was on the floor and Pop's usually tan torso, was a bright pink. The plaster had sweat bleached his tan and had near made him raw. Mom slathered his body with Aunt Cora Munn's homemade All Purpose Salve. The family used the salve for almost any ailment, and it always worked. No one ever knew what was in it, but it was potent.

Things then turned to a whirlwind of activity as we helped Pop get dressed. Mom packed his suitcase with clothes for a week away. Our big sister was busy filling a big paper poke with vittles for dad to eat. Soon everything was in order.

Like a herd of buffalo we all followed Pop to the car. Suitcase and bag on the front seat beside him. Hugs and kisses. He gingerly slid behind the wheel, starter grinding and the car came alive. Neighbors have come out to send him off with a wave and good wishes. Pop closed the door, put the car in gear and with a wave he was off.

He was in pain for weeks surviving mostly on aspirin and whiskey, but mostly just ignoring the pain and working through it. That's the way my parents' generation were, seldom frantic, mostly in control.

Pop healed and went on to live well into his eighties. Interestingly enough about three years ago I fell and broke my back... Harkening to lessons learned, I'm mostly ignoring the pain and focusing on being in control of what needs to be done. I'm not of the Greatest Generation, but I inherited some of their skills and fortitude.

Today this all would seem unbearable. Each of us come from strong stock. We've been weakened by the generally accepted thoughts that we will be taken care of by others. Insurance plans, government programs and charitable groups are reaching out to help us in time of need. We can dial 911 and have police protection or the EMTs to help us, or transported to an ER. Most of us live in a nation where we are well protected.

But at what cost? Do we actually have what it takes to work through pain, do what's necessary and to take care of ourselves? First answer would be yes, but thinking deeply, are you really capable of taking care of yourself like the Greatest Generation did?

It's time for each of us to dig deep and discover our basic survival skills, and determine what we need to learn to expand those, to cover any situation. Like the apple, we have not fallen far from the tree... but we have gotten lazy, and I dare say, careless.

Aspire to be like those in your grandparents era. What stories can you recall from folks of that generation? Can you develop your skills to be a person of whom they would be proud? Try channeling their innate abilities, to be the best they could be, and follow those examples.

Like them, you too can be of your own "greatest generation."

- 25 -
Ribbons in the Sky

Do you have a Bucket List? Things you want to see, do, accomplish, places you want to visit before you... pardon the phrase... "Kick the bucket"?

The idea was made really popular in 2007 when the movie of the same name was released. It drew attention to the desire to do and experience something out of the ordinary, something memorable, something you've always wanted to do, and don't want to leave this life *before* you do.

I have not compiled an official list yet (although I found some fascinating websites that will help you do so!) but I do have some basics in mind. In fact, I had one I honestly never dreamed I would be able to fulfill – mostly due to my own aversion to the cold and unwillingness to spend any more time in it than has been necessary.

The Northern Lights (Aurora Borealis) have always fascinated me. It seems pure magic, a fantasy vision, to see ribbons of light rippling across a night sky. Neon green, deep pink, cobalt blue, royal purple... Something so dynamic, silently sailing above.

Before I traveled to Sweden in my teens, and long before there was anything like the internet to help with research, I had the idea that Sweden must be far enough north to be able to see them. Wrong. At least where I was visiting, anyway. It was far too much south for any such display.

For the rest of my adult years I didn't give it too much thought. I spent my mid-life scheming how to get out of the cold winters of Ohio, permanently, and never had any desire to vacation to a place colder than where I already was! The romantic notion of seeing the Northern Lights just faded away to the distant background.

Thirty five years passed by. We had since moved to the desert, away from the cold Ohio winters, and our dream of an Alaskan cruise became a reality. Even as we embarked on this great adventure, I had not yet resurrected the Northern Lights dream, assuming we would still be too far south.

To my immense delight, on our first day the Captain announced that, outside of Juneau, we would very likely be able to see the Northern Lights. I squeaked with surprise and excitement. Like a little child, I waited patiently for the night to arrive.

And waited. And waited. Just as we were crawling into bed for the night, the telltale Captain's alert tones came across the speakers.

"Wakey wakey, everyone! This is your captain, Captain Alex, talking to you from the bridge!" This was in a singsong voice, as we had come to find delightful... Alex Papadopoulos really enjoyed his job, his enthusiasm was infectious and so heartwarming! "We have spotted some Northern Lights ahead of us and are going to be slowing the ship for you to go out and see. Everyone out on your balconies and out on deck! It is a Northern Lights pajama party!!"

I sprung from my bed and threw on every warm piece of clothing I could find, flung open the slider and scrambled out on the balcony.

We stood there, looking up into the cold black Alaskan night sky. As our eyes adjusted, looking off to our left towards the front of the ship, we began to see ribbons of neon green. Fleeting... almost imperceptible... and then they came brighter and clearer.

The captain slowed the ship to a near stop and shut off all but emergency lighting outdoors so we had the best chance to see and take photos.

I caught my breath. I hadn't realized how much I had been anticipating this moment... for so many years. Instant tears in my eyes, and more emotion that I would ever have guessed, took me totally by surprise.

Silent waving ribbons in the sky. Neon green. Appearing and disappearing in the fog. Mysterious. Ethereal. Magical. Seemed like something that majestic should have some sonic accompaniment but... nothing. Silence. The silence made it all the more spine tingling.

We stayed until they were lost behind the increasing fog. Shivering, I made my way back to bed.

Imagine! A bucket list item crossed off the list... just like that. Actually... two. I'd always wanted to see Alaska by cruise, too.

I will never forget that night. And I think that's what Bucket List items must be – something so extraordinary that it leaves with you an everlasting feeling and memory so strong it stands out amongst others.

What's on your Bucket List? Do you have one? If you don't, what will you add to it? If you do, what's keeping you from checking off those items?

People have a need to dream, to aspire to more than what and where they currently are. We want to accomplish things that make us happy, make us feel good about ourselves, and provide us with experiences that will give us lifelong memories.

If you don't have the Bucket List, consider starting one. If you do, review it often. Decide on the next item you will set out to achieve.

Without a solid Vision, we cannot hope to achieve our goals and dreams. We must speak it, see it, plan for it, and then do it.

Go see the Grand Canyon, learn a new language, volunteer at a charity and change someone's life.

Do it.

And when you do... please write to the WeWan and let us know how it felt. Send us pictures. I want to know that you're happy and achieving your dreams. Only you can accomplish for yourself.

Drew Book
Sugar Grove, Scioto County, OH

- 26 -
Drew Book, Common Man's Artist

America has always been imbued with the spirit of entrepreneurship. Whether it was John Paul Jones as a silversmith, Benjamin Franklin as a printer, to Henry Ford and his fabulous assembly line – many great luminaries in our history have started out with the desire to be their own boss. The spirit has kept us strong throughout all of our nation's history, where the small business is the backbone of the American economy.

The entrepreneurial drive was never limited to the successful and wealthy. Every town, village and city, along every by-way and up every holler, men and women alike created products to share with their neighbors.

My particular elders must have been well inoculated with that spirit, for nearly every elder and ancestor in my lineage have, at one time or another, been in business for themselves. In this book I share many stories of such people, from my grandparents and aunts and uncles to my father, always looking for a great business to put food on the table... and to add a few extra coins in his pocket.

From wheelwrights to car dealerships, country markets to grocery stores, roadside stands to restaurants, and even snake oil potions to healing salves... that actually worked. If there were a market, someone in my family would strive to fill that need.

One of the unique small businessmen in my family was my first cousin, A. J. Drew Book (1905-1981). He was the eldest of five children. I don't know a lot about cousin Drew, other than what I remember as a child, and the stories passed down through the family. My first recollection was his house on the river side of US 52, in the little wide spot in the road... Ziegler's Lane. There were a whole passel of family living in that small community. My Aunt Cora and Uncle Floyd Munn lived on the riverfront Bluffs at the end of the lane, the Comptons, and other shoestring relatives lived all along the road paralleling the mighty Ohio River. It was a special place to visit, and we always had family to keep us company.

Cousin Drew was unique – Drew could draw... and then paint. That was his great skill. He had a natural eye, not that he was a Rembrandt or Michelangelo, but he was our family's equivalent to the self-taught country primitive artists. He was our Grandma Moses... a true American folk artist.

My cousin Tonette Venturino Howbert shared... "I stood and watched Uncle Drew paint many times. He was so amazing and quick with his talent. He used to practice his sermons sometimes as he painted."

I remember visiting his home with Gram and going to his workshop out in front of his home. We ate fried chicken many times with them after church. Aunt Lil was a terrific cook. It was always a family affair.

I can't tell you how many times I stood inside his shop and browsed stacks and stacks of his canvasses. Each was a true work of art. His ability to paint woodland creatures, the Ohio hills and the beauty of the change of seasons would take my breath away. Waterfalls, rivers, flora & fauna were always present.

Cousin Drew was a well known artist in the region, and his works are in collections across the nation today.

In the time between the World Wars rural and small town people – where jobs were hard to find – had to be ingenious in creating cash products. Every family in these areas has stories about their talented and determined entrepreneurs, who oftentimes through necessity created a myriad of small businesses.

In today's marketplace, the small business is still the backbone of our economy. The adage, "find a niche to fill, and create a product to fill it," still applies.

- 27 -
Rollercoasters and Death Drops

For as long as I can remember, my mother always loved rollercoasters. When I was very young, she would take me to a local amusement park for kids. Kiddie Park, in Brooklyn, Ohio. It had a great array of pint-sized rides. There were flat ones, fast ones, slow ones, spinny ones and, of course, a rollercoaster, "The Little Dipper." It was a great introduction to the joys of such entertainment.

As they say, it's all fun and games until...

In this case, "until" was me getting tall enough to ride the adult rides at the big amusement parks, of which we had two great ones relatively close to where we lived, Geauga Lake and Cedar Point.

I recall vividly my mother trying to introduce me to the "thrill" of rollercoasters. Not fun. Not fun at all. For me. For her, she was having a rip-roaring good time!

Now keep in mind the time period here. It's the mid 1970's as I was just getting tall enough to participate in this strange activity of scaring oneself silly, laughing insanely about it, and then repeating it! In "those days," the rollercoasters were usually wooden and simply a stomach-dropping sequence of hills, hairpin turn, more hills, screeching halt, jump out (and get back in line). Lap bars only. No loopy twisty turn-you-upside-down steel coasters that require over the shoulder harnesses to keep the willing (or not) participant in their seat.

Even so, those early days of mom and me on wooden coasters was enough to scare the bejeebers out of me. I could not understand why this was fun. Up, down, up, down, and the feeling of coming off the seat a little with just that lap bar to hang on to...

Incomprehensible how this could be fun for anybody. Nope, I just wasn't "diggin' it."

Fast forward ten years. Now in my teens and my high school buddies want to make a summer day trip to Cedar Point in Sandusky, Ohio. I'm all in. I love rides (that weren't coasters). Anything spinny especially. The spinnier (that's not really a word but it's descriptive, no?) the more I loved it. No motion sickness, nothing.

Then the inevitable happened... they wanted to go on all the newfangled crazy steel coasters *and* the wooden ones. All of it. Oy! Luckily I didn't hang around with people who were into peer pressure. Quite the opposite, they respected my "fear," and gave me my space. At the same time, they really tried to convince me it was perfectly safe – and if I wanted to try, they'd hold my hand, etc., etc.

I had *great* high school friends! And...

Eventually they convinced me to try it.

Who knew it could be so much fun?! All those years I'd been missing out! My new opinion: Rollercoasters ROCKED. Just like that. I don't know what changed but it did. And now I was addicted and understood why my mother loved it so much. Thanks, mom!! Thanks, high school buddies!!

We spent that summer day trying every single rollercoaster in the park. And there were many in the mid 1980s. Some we rode more than once. All this in addition to all the spinny rides we could squeeze in between. And the swingy ones, too.

It was a great day because I was with my friends and we had fun together. It was an even better day because I'd conquered a fear and realized that the feared thing had never been worth all the anxiety I'd wasted on it.

Fast forward another *thirty* years this time. Now I've been married a good long time, and hadn't been to an amusement park in quite a while. Sadly, I've learned that rides that spin are no longer on my fun menu. Dangit. Age can be so cruel. It somehow disallowed me from spinning excessively without nausea. Now? Green. Ugh.

So off to every rollercoaster we could find, and enjoy most of them we did. Nothing like making the best of what you've got, right?

At the end of the day, my husband asked me for the hundredth time to please try the "death drop" type ride he loves so much.

The first of this kind many years previous had been called Demon Drop... apropos, in my humble opinion. I (really!) didn't like it in the 90s, I couldn't understand what would have changed.

That's a lie. I *did know*. Here's what changed: rather than being harnessed neatly in to a big metal box which was cut out in the front, the seats were now "hung" on the outside of a ring that ran up and down a very (very very) tall tower.

This was insanity. Who in their right minds found this sort of thing amusing? And "best" of all, they now gave you a choice: shoot you up fast and then you drift down, or slowly raise you up, and then *shoot* you back down to earth. Oh, yippee. Nuts, I tell you.

But my husband has always been the type to insist and insist so... what the hell... I'll try it once and then we're leaving. Agreed? Agreed.

And off we go to wait in a relatively short line. (Because how many people can be crazy enough to do this sort of thing?!) And I had to make a choice – shoot up/drift down, or slow pull up/shoot down.

Would I like to die from a heart attack on the way up or the way down? That's basically what it came to.

I chose to go up slow and drop down fast. I thought that was the closest thing to "rollercoaster."

Our turn came and we chose seats, got ourselves strapped, harnessed, *clamped* onto this tiny little perch which was nothing more than a bicycle seat welded onto a ring of steel. And the time was now...

Up, up, up we went. Slowly. Painfully slowly. While I was losing my mind in the two hours it took to get to the top (I'm exaggerating!), Bryan was encouraging me to gaze out onto the scene below. We could see all of the park, the entirety of Lake Erie and half of Canada (again, I exaggerate).

And then they just hung us there. Another two hours. Ok, it felt like it. Legs dangling in mid air 200 feet above the earth.

And just like that... whoosh! Down we fell.

What a rush! No joke! It was amazing. Legs flew out, hair flew up, stomachs hit the backs of our throats, and then we were back down at ground level. Amazing really.

Once again, I was surprised at my thrill. I discovered I loved the adrenalin rush. We got unstrapped and immediately ran back in line for another go.

How can one have such a love/hate relationship with fear? It seems wholly unnatural. But on further exploration, it's the most natural thing, really. Fight or flight. Run away... Or confront and conquer. Opposite sides of the same coin.

Many of us love to be scared. Amusement park rides, like in the story I just told you. Haunted houses. Scary books and movies.

Others love the more real challenge of rock climbing, race car driving, deep sea diving. In those activities, the participants follow strict protocol to make it as unlikely as possible that fun thrill will turn to real danger.

The caveat in those scenarios is that it's only fun when we are pretty confident that it isn't – or won't turn – real. Adrenalin with mitigation. Danger with a safety net.

Some call it adrenalin addiction, especially when we feel compelled to repeat the exposure to fear/danger. However, it can be a way for us to cope with the anxiety that fear can bring. Every time we do something that scares us, and succeed, we are bolstered in our confidence.

To do or not to do is obviously a personal choice. But the key word is choice. Don't linger and agonize over the decision.

Engaging in prolonged anxiety and fear – e.g., deliberating whether to participate or walk away – is a drain on us. It's exhausting. We better serve ourselves and our future by making a decision and following through. Over-deliberation leads to vacillating on choices and eventually it all becomes too confusing to move forward.

Weigh the options well and when you are out of arguments decide yay or nay and move forward. And remember that every time you face a fear, and discover it's not as scary as you thought, you have won a victory for yourself.

Lingering too long on the edge of a steel ring perched on a bicycle seat gets to be less fun every moment. Take the plunge. Mom knew what she was doing by introducing me to thrill rides!

Great House
Urbana, OH

– 28 –
Pop and the Women Elders at the Great House

My dad, Chief Ten Moons – *Okema Metathwe Dekeelswa* – began attending Shawnee tribal events in central Ohio during the 1970s but never was much interested in the ceremonial aspects of tribal life.

Many will recall him at Red Fox Camp as he sat in the shade of the great mighty oaks and shared stories of another time with our children. Stories of when he was a child like them. This was a teaching time for the youngsters as well as many adults who had never heard these stories. They became mature children sitting at his feet. He wove his tales of times long past, forgotten by all but the Elders. He used these stories to teach history and culture, both of which have been mostly lost within our modern educational system. He spun his stories into fables, always with multiple learning points, that entertained, beguiled and educated those who listened. Many of the children, now adults, have shared with me how his stories changed their lives for the better.

For nearly all of the twentieth century, my father was filled with the greatness of change that had occurred. He spoke often of his fascination with having been born in the day of the horse and buggy, and steam paddle wheelers on the Ohio River region. He was filled with the wonder of scientific discoveries and society's evolution. From the dust along the dirt trail to Turtle Mountain, to the precious moon rocks brought home by his modern heroes, he was charged with its wonder.

Through all this, he had ridden two horses – one red and the other white. One, of the traditions and honors of his Indian ancestors – and the other, charged with his European forefathers' never-ending quest for the new. Mounted with a foot firmly planted on the back of each horse, he kept his balance throughout. My father made no compromise. The world of his youth, rooted in history and tradition had to accept the challenge of the "unbelievable changes that had occurred" in his lifetime.

Telephones, radios, and television enchanted him. He marveled at the communication explosion, was awed at how the world had become so small. It challenged belief that a trip to the far corners of the earth that would have taken weeks and months when he was a young lad, could now be made in but a matter of hours. The span of his life must have been truly spectacular.

For a decade or more my dad would sit down by the community house, cup of black coffee in hand, and watch. For him it was a time to rest between the storytelling and the evening's potlatch. He often just watched the birds as they flew in the sky…. Reminding him of the biplanes of his early days. Birds like kites and planes like birds filled his eyes against the blue sky while his mind drifted to other times in other places. He truly enjoyed those moments.

Year after year the people gathered together in traditional wear, preparing to practice the ancient ceremonial traditions. They would be lively with chatter and excitement and as they passed my dad, many would invite him to join them. He would always graciously decline.

It wasn't until much later, after watching the majority of people make the processional walk across the Prairie and towards the Great House, that his interest was piqued. He had often been to the Great House, helping repair or add to the sacred lodge. He was a skilled craftsman. But he never attended any of the ceremonies.

The people found this most peculiar as he was a revered Elder and Wisdom Keeper. Of all the people, why didn't he participate in our ceremonies? The question was always in the minds but was never, to my knowledge, asked of him… Out of respect.

Year after year, he would sit on the bench next to the community building and watch the grand procession move away to perform our ancient cultural traditions. As he began his eighth decade, he started showing some interest. That next spring as the procession moved towards the ancient lodge, he at last decided it. He joined the last of the people to walk up to the ceremonial area.

The Great House, or *Chisakewin Wicon*, they approached was a spectacular pre-Colombian Shawnee-style construction. The principal structure in the compound resembled a giant upside down basket. Nearly thirty feet across and fifteen feet at its peak, the circular lodge walls consisted of living trees with sturdy branches and vines. The roof was supported by four center poles and covered with bark shingles except over the altar in the east. The surrounding smaller lodges were for the men and the women, and the ceremonial leaders. All in all it was a most impressive site. It did great honor to our ancestors.

Taking a chair near the processional entrance to our Holy Place, where he could hear the Ceremonies taking place inside, he determined that this was as close as he could get, and still remain outside the Great House proper.

This reoccured over a couple years, and was a puzzlement to all, including family members.

Eventually the Women's Council decided to take matters into their own hands, and despite a great amount of resistance, they were able to escort him just inside the entrance of the lodge, where he would sit on the very end of the bench.

Here the Holy People would bring him the various elements of the ritual, the Pipe, token meal and other traditional sacred symbols. I can only recall once when he actually circumambulated the full ceremony.

In the fall of his 83rd year, he was asked by the Sachem why he was so reluctant to enter the ceremonial lodge, and later still refused to fully participate in our rituals. His answer astounded them.

He felt unworthy because he had denied his heritage much of his life.

Following this acknowledgment, he found peace within. He had atoned for his shame and had returned to the tribal rituals he had so long denied himself.

At the closing of his life, and the unfolding dawn of a heavenly tomorrow, his mind had returned to the innocence and magic of his youth. He passed through the Veil in the winter of his 88th year.

As the Shawnee/Mide' Clan gathered on the top of the hill around the freshly dug hole in the sand, it was one last time for remembrance. We had carried the body of our father, first by caravan to this outlook above the Ohio River, and now by hand to this burial place, where so many of our ancestors remains lay.

It had turned gray and icy in the valley the Iroquois named Ohio, the "Beautiful Place." Sleet driven hard by the bitter cold winds of the First Snow Moon cut our flesh, reminding those gathered that we had not yet begun our final journey.

To the east, "Wee-lo! Wee-lo! Wee-lo! We send you our Great Chief," the Sachem called out... Again towards the south... "We send you our beloved." Looking into the west, down the long gray ribbon of river where the old Chief and his mother had often contemplated upon days' end, the Sachem offered: "We send you our cherished father." Once more he turned. Now the sound reverberated north, deep into the ancient hills as he spoke those sacred words a last time. "Wee-lo! Wee-lo! Wee-lo! We give you the care of your brother Chief Ten Moons," and they echoed into chilled silence.

Adean, the ceremonies were concluded.

It was his way through life that the important things be properly attended to. One could but smile at the thought, that even during this time he had "covered all his bases."

He lived well and full the measure he met, to outlive his chums was his only regret. The tears had dried and the cold again cut hard, as the reality of the moment returned with the bitter winter winds to these Woodland People. Yes, it was a time to remember, a time to recall our Shawandasse Babackis'iganatuk-

Okema Metathwe Dekeelswa (Shawnee Elder-Chief Ten Moons). He was born just thirty miles east of that knoll on October 30th, four years into the twentieth century.

He had seen his world change from wagons and horses, buffalo and elk, to a world he could never have dreamed. His last recollections in this life were of his earliest times. He recalled his first school, the Turtle Mountain Territorial School, and the trip there by covered wagon. He remembered the remnants of the great herds of buffalo and the first motorcar he encountered. He told stories of the hard but honest life of his youth; and spoke always of his father and mother, his brother, and all their friends now long gone.

For nearly as many seasons as days in the year, he had walked on his cherished Grandmother Earth. He had poured his cup to the brim and had filled his being with the grandness of life. But he was the last of his generation. He was his own "Ishi." No longer could anyone reminisce the glory of his youth, and he missed that, to the center of his being. The Tribe and the Clan of his time were gone. And now it was his time to join All His Relations.

He closed his eyes to this place just days after he had marked his eighty-eighth year. He passed through with the First Snow Moon of the ninety-second year of his century. It had been a grand adventure.

We do not feel the bitterness of the absence of our Brother/Father Chief Ten Moons, but sing often songs of happiness. And retell to you the stories he imparted, for that should be his greatest legacy, his gift from the ancestors, our unchanged sacred oral tradition. The remembered word, the spoken history throughout the hundreds of generations

His passing is as with all mortals, his words shared are the living reality of our Ancestors.

Old Rotary Phone

- 29 -
The Only Way Out Is Through

When I was much younger, having to make a telephone call (outside of friends or family) was a fate worse than death. I would do *anything* – anything! – to get out of having to do it. I dreaded even the thought of it. I mean, *dreaded* it. Verging on phobia kind of fear. I would avoid it at all costs. Pleading with others to make the call for me. Finding excuses why I didn't really have to. I was a master of avoidance via abject terror.

And the fear was founded, in my opinion. Whenever I got on the phone for some specified purpose – anything from checking on a library book to making a dinner reservation – I froze. My tongue froze. I stammered and stumbled. And it seemed the more I tried, the worse it got. My failures made me more and more paranoid. It got to the point that I would literally lose my breath and start to tremble at the prospect of making a call.

In my household and family, it became a bit of a joke. Don't dare ask Kelly to make a phone call, she'll pass out. However, I was encouraged to keep trying – mom and aunt both gave me very useful tips and encouraged me lovingly – but nothing seemed to help me calm down and just do it. I even tried writing down everything I must remember to say so that when I froze in fear, I could have a cheat sheet to put me back on track.

In 1981, ninth grade, I was fortunate enough to be selected to test for entry into an exclusive group of independent schools. That in itself is a story for another time. The short of it is that I was accepted into the one I longed for the most. It was an incredibly exciting time. However… it did not come with a scholarship and so my family was left to ponder how my mother would afford it and who could do what to help her.

My aunt had wonderful employers, who were also very supportive of excellent education. They generously offered me a job working in their office over summer breaks to help me pay for part of my tuition. Honestly, it was a cushy job and the money was verging on obscene – but my aunt Marlene had worked there for decades and was now a Vice President. It had perks. The job responsibilities meant I had to answer the phone when the other ladies in the office were not available to do so. Ok, no problem, I could always *receive* calls with no problem. It was *making* them that sent me into fits.

And then the day came when I actually had to learn to use the intercom/company speaker system. It was one of those moments where you realize no matter how afraid you are, *not* doing something will be worse for you than just doing it. So I just did it. Not very gracefully. But...

I survived it. And I made mistakes but I didn't *die* from paging someone to the front waiting room to greet guests!

As I became more comfortable with my responsibilities there, I was trusted with more tasks. Inevitably, I had to make phone calls. *Gasp!* Perhaps it started simply as one day having to order lunch for the office staff. I don't recall the *exact* impetus. Suffice to say whatever it was, again I had to face it or be at risk of refusing to do a part of my job. As they say now, I had to put my big girl panties on and just get through it.

Much to my amazement, I discovered some months later that I didn't even think about picking up the phone anymore. I just did it. Sometimes I made notes to myself before I dialed – I actually do that still today if it's a really important call and has many points I must address.

All these years later, I have no such fear. In fact, the joke in my family now is that "Kelly is way better on the phone, ask her to call them." And I will admit to agreeing far more times than not.

You see, I've gotten it down to an art. There is no one on the other end of that phone that can intimidate me now. My confidence has grown, and I have carefully nurtured a style of strength and credibility through humility and conviviality. By the end of the most dreaded and stressful calls – even those when I am really raging and upset before I dial – I am usually smiling and laughing and expressing graciousness for the help I am given.

The phone is not mine enemy, only I can be.

Examine your fears and find the path to walk through them.

The fear I felt when I was young as it related to making phone calls was real. And it was debilitating. Imagine how my adult life would have developed if I had not been forced to walk through the fear and get out on the other side of it?

Sometimes the only way out is walking straight through, head held high, and confident as you can be. When you get to the other side, you will breathe a sigh of relief and look behind you. You will see that the thing you fear so greatly was something conquerable, not something that will continue to plague you.

The next time you are really dreading something, promise yourself that you will have the courage to endure and get through it. Nothing lasts forever, even the things we fear the most... although it can certainly feel like it will.

Do what you can to prepare yourself – practice, make notes, visualize. Developing tools of coping with the fear and supporting a positive outcome will build your confidence in yourself. When you've conquered the fear, however many times you must do so to banish it, you will find you are now very sure of yourself in that area.

- 30 -
"See Fred Brown!"

The remarkable men and women of the Greatest Generation have been a continual well-source that has guided me throughout my life. I have been privileged to sit in the shadow of some truly remarkable folk. These extraordinary people were all around me when I was a child.

At the country store, I listened to the spit-n-chew club gathered around the potbelly stove, spinning tales and telling in a common voice, feats of extraordinary valor and commitment.

My elders would sit around in overstuffed furniture reminiscing, after enjoying another feast at one family or another's gatherings. Many were the times when we would sit on the bench in front of my grandparents' restaurant, listening to the locals, as they spoke of every day life along the Ohio River, down in Appalachia.

Each of these remarkable people in their own way imprinted me, my siblings and the youth of my generation. We could only hope to be as successful at imparting our wisdom as they were with us. For the most part, they are gone... now it is our responsibility to recall, and pass on the bits of wisdom that they shared with us.

This is one of those stories.

One of the most remarkable characters from that era, who impacted me in many ways, was my Uncle Fred Brown. He married my mom's kid sister, Ruth, and together they created a series of businesses that brought them wealth and fame.

Uncle Fred was a war hero. He was a Marine in World War II in the South Pacific Arena where he was wounded and awarded the Purple Heart. He came out of World War II with a small G.I. disability.

Returning home he took his first disability check of $25, found an old used car and a can of paint. He beat out the dents, sanded it down... and with house paint and a brush, he made her look new and shiny. He parked it out in the front yard of his home with a "For Sale" sign on it.

Sold it in a day.

Taking the profit from the sale, he bought other cars, repaired them, painted them and sold them from his front yard. Soon his reputation grew as a reliable fella from whom to buy good running, restored, used vehicles... not only sedans, but work trucks too. Folks would say, "Go see Fred for a great deal!"

Fred attended the General Motors Technology Institute and, in 1953, opened a Cadillac dealership in Portsmouth. He was the youngest Cadillac dealer in the world at that time. Capitalizing on his name, he named his new dealership... C. Fred Brown! That was not a stretch, as his full name was Charles Fredrick Brown... "See Fred Brown!"

From this humble beginning, selling Cadillacs and Oldsmobiles, he became a tri-state dealer for these products. Soon his business was thriving. His dealership lasted for decades. Some of the older residents of the area still recall buying their cars from "Fred."

During that time he was also building another business, finding and restoring high priced collectible automobiles. First he sourced areas in the states for barn finds and "lightly" wrecked (fabulous) old cars. Overseas, he would scour the back roads and towns of Europe buying entire ship loads of quality cars. Name it and he bought it... all quality vehicles. Load theming on freighters he shipped them across the Atlantic, up the St. Lawrence seaway to Cleveland, Ohio. Then he transported them by truck to a facility just to the south of Columbus, Ohio.

The business was so successful that he was able to build a large factory where the damaged vehicles would be brought in the door at one end, placed on a dolly and, moving through the various stations, cleaning out the chicken feathers and muck, to the body shop where the metal was restored to pristine condition. Next the engine and drivetrain were restored and tuned to perfection, then to the paint department for a bright shiny spray... and finally to the detailers. The process made each vehicle a vision to behold. Every car was restored to their original state. Some of the top rated show cars in Concours de Elegance events worldwide came from his "factory."

Fred's interest and expertise in classic luxury cars eventually led him to specialize in Rolls Royce and Bentleys. It was so successful, Fred and Ruth were able to travel extensively in Europe and England, pursuing their interests.

They retired in 1982 and moved to Paradise Valley, Arizona in 1987. Fred, an avid golfer, joined the Camelback Country Club and became a 'regular' – he participated in tournaments and was proud of his three "Hole-in-Ones." Fred and Ruth loved animals. He was supportive of his wife's show dogs, but always had his own big dog that accompanied him everywhere.

Like many of his military chums, back from the war, he was able to become a highly successful businessman that made him a millionaire. In his final years, he and my aunt lived high. Throughout his life, he never forgot his humble country roots... work hard, smart and persevere.

His advice was always welcomed.

One time when I had asked him to invest with me in a whiz-bang cockamamie pyramid scheme, he admonished me to never partner with anyone unless it was a 50/50 partnership. Never give away equal control of your money, status and power to anyone. And then he said, "Sorry Jimmie, your deal violates my core principles, and these folks are working a con."

He could see a con a mile away, and his counsel and advice have stood me well from that time on.

My aunt and uncle shared a 50-50 partnership in their businesses throughout their lives. My aunt helped him as he grew his car business, and he helped her as she grew her business of breeding and showing dogs – and acquiring a room full of ribbons and trophies in the process. They always had each other's back. God help the person that would cross them. They were a dynamic duo.

The depression and World War II made some very savvy people, the same people who grew us out of the terrible depression days of the 1930's, and lead us to victory against the Nazis, Fascists, Socialists and Imperialist in the 1940's.

Yet another reason we know them as the Greatest Generation.

Wise people today could learn form their innate wisdom, perseverance, common sense and intuitiveness... and their "trust but verify" way of life.

They were Folks worthy of our admiration, and imitation.

- 31 -
They Come in the Wind

The sacred teachings of the Midewiwin are esoteric at best. The old Shawnee medicine path of the Four Levels of the Earth and Sky is almost extinct these days. Only a few of us are left to teach, and even fewer of us to express a desire to learn, and possess the fortitude, to pursue entrance, and achieve, all eight levels.

The study of Mide' requires one to pursue very specific assignments at each level. As we begin the Third Level of the Earth and of the Sky, we turn our attention to more esoteric ideas. It is at this time that we are told by our teacher – our Mide' – to discover the magic. And to begin by listening for the voices of the Ancestors.

It's a simple statement. Short and to the point. "Listen for the voices of the Ancestors."

In my case, I had absolutely no idea what it meant. I'm a city girl, born and raised. Educated as an engineer, trained to think objectively and logically. This assignment "did not compute."

I had so many questions.

"What am I listening for? *Who* am I listening for?"

"How will I know?"

"What will they say?"

The answer from my own Mide' was no surprise. It was the one that usually frustrates me the most. "You'll know it when it happens."

So I waited. And listened. And felt like I was pulling on a push door.

I must be forthright with you, however. This was not as foreign to me as perhaps I make it out to be. As a child, I "saw" things not infrequently. But because it was a bit uncomfortable for one or two of my family members to be told that someone they couldn't see had just walked through the room, I was quietly discouraged from sharing... and eventually, I also stopped "receiving." That part of me drifted away and I grew up and accepted critical thinking and logic as my way of life.

Now to have found my way back to thinking there was more to this world than math and science... More than only what we can see and touch... it took me awhile to figure out what I thought of that, really. My heart told me to open up and find out what happened next.

A long time passed. Months went by. And, as the assignment's frustrating elements quieted to a "wait and see" patience, my world began to change.

It started with waking "visions" and dreams during sleep that were too specific and profound to be dismissed as mere somnolent brain chatter. Messages seemed to be there – and more importantly, answers to questions I had asked.

As I acknowledged them, one by one, I found myself opening to more. This was not me "making stuff up." Or wishful thinking. My experiences were specific and relevant, they were attention-getting... increasingly so. And yet still I felt like I was missing the definitive experience, the one that would allow me to believe I really could hear the Ancestors at will.

On a cold November day, in rural western Ohio near the Indiana border, I attended ceremony with my People and spent social time with them as I always did. Sheltered from the cold in our community building, we shared a meal, and conversation. It was how we always were with one another, all of us, enjoying one another's company and mentally preparing for the long winter nights ahead.

In a private conversation, I confided to my closest tribal sisters what was weighing so heavily on my heart that evening. As they always did, they gave good counsel, advising me to take my question to the Ancestors in the Great House and listen closely for their response. "Magic happens in the Great House," they told me. "Go see for yourself."

With bright full moonlight as my only guide, I walked the path to the Great House. My Mide' accompanied me, I so needed to not be alone during this. I asked permission from the Ancestors to enter and went to sit by the dying ceremonial fire. It remained warm, sparks flying once in a while. The night was still and the scene was almost surreal. Silver moonlight bathed everything – the fire pit, the tall lodge pole, the altar, the benches, walls made of cut tree branches, the mud pit, even the grass underfoot. All shone in a black and white scene – brilliant clarity, like the old nitrate films of yesteryear. Natural things having been arranged by the hand of humans for the purpose of connecting to the Creator.

I determined to sit quietly, asking earnestly for help, for some message, some answer to resolving the intense pain that was in my heart that night. Eventually enough time passed that my incessant brain chatter quieted, and I was left with just me, sitting in the Great House, waiting for something. I had no clue what it was. I trusted my Elders that I "would know it when it happened."

I began to feel a bit ridiculous. I started to think that maybe this sort of thing would never happen for me, that perhaps I was just not ready yet, had not done the right things to prepare… or maybe what I closed off in childhood was closed permanently, never to be resurrected.

Thinking that maybe I should leave and chalk it up to bad timing, I got up and knelt at the almost-cold ceremonial fire, pleading one last time for help. And I waited just a moment more, listening.

And then it happened.

From a perfectly still and calm night came a whoosh of wind so great it could not be mistaken for anything but the arrival of the help I sought. And I heard them. Voices. Whispering, murmuring. The wind whipped around me, buffeting me and hugging me at the same time. It was Them. The Ancestors had come at last to counsel me. As I had grown accustomed from my teacher, the message was very simple, and crystal clear. And surprisingly, it was an experience as if someone were physically speaking to me.

For the sake of my family's privacy, I will refrain from being specific about the exact words they spoke. Suffice to say, it was pointed, brief, and left me without doubt that I had a direct answer to my inquiry.

As soon as I had the message, they were gone. The wind died down and the night was once again still. From behind me I heard my Mide''s voice, "What just happened?" I was crying but I also smiled. "I just heard my answer. They came."

From that point on, when I have had need of counsel from beyond this Turtle Island, I ask and then wait for the Wind. For me, They always come in the Wind, my guides, my Ancestors. The wind brings their Voices to me, and amplifies them so I might hear clearly.

And, as most people do when they get to the other side of education on a topic, I learned that the advice given me was absolutely true... I knew when it happened. It was beyond doubt. It was a definitive experience.

I also learned that in order to "hear," one must be quiet. Truly and deeply quiet. We cannot expect to receive answers when we are too busy filling ourselves with our own thoughts and voice.

They come in the Wind.

Quiet yourself, and listen carefully. They will be there for you when you are in need. All you need do is open yourself to Them.

- 32 -
THE DAY I STOPPED THE PIPE

"It is faith that is older than dirt. It is the ceremonies and rituals which have been built upon from history and the beginning of our creation from the centers of the world, wherever we may find them. And it is not for sale!!!" ~ Dakota Spiritual Man, Little Crow Bryant.

It's funny how one person's heritage or tradition, although it would seem to be similar to others, is so diametrically different. Point in case, the Native American Pipe Ceremony.

Every weekend at a school in Orange County, Little Crow held American Indian Church Gatherings. The weekly message that Little Crow brought, "There is no Bible, no sin, no conversion." The Gathering was a nondenominational Native American church that met with no written text, only a message of responsibility, truth, and a faith that all things, great and small, are sacred and interconnected... and a spiritual Pipe Ceremony based in the Dakota tradition.

Even so, great respect was rendered to the many different nations represented in the congregation. There were Hopi, Apache, Comanche, Cherokee and many different representatives of the California Mission Indians. I am a descendent of the Eastern Woodland Shawnee People, and our traditions are similar to other tribes in many ways, but also diverse. This was the case the day I, inadvertently, stopped the pipe.

I had been a regular attendee at the weekly gatherings, and most there knew that I was a Pipe Carrier for my people. Because I was not of Dakota heritage, I respectfully sat outside the Circle, honoring their tradition. One Sunday morning, a representative of the Circle asked me if I would participate. Of course I was honored and would do my best to respect their Pipe Ceremony. I had never done a Dakota ceremony, but paid close attention that I may honor this day.

Little Crow's book, "From the Gathering," offers, "*As long as that Pipe is connected, everything we think, say or do... goes through that Pipe and out into the universe... and it affects everything else in the universe. That's what the Pipe means, that's what it is about. It is paying homage and respect to our creation.*"

The Pipe that day, as every time, was prepared for the ceremony by Little Crow. Taking a pinch of sacred tobacco he placed it in the bowl while facing the four cardinal directions and to Grandfather Sky and Grandmother Earth. This continued, adding a pinch of sacred tobacco with the same ritual. At last the pipe was prepared to be lit. As Little Crow so often said, "Don't use any old zippo to light a Ceremonial Pipe. That's disrespectful!" This day was no exception. One of the acolytes brought in an abalone shell with smoldering embers of sacred herbs. Touching a piece of grass straw to the ember, Little Crow ignited it – thereby using a piece of nature to light the Pipe, as is the tradition.

After he had completed the lighting ritual, he again offered the sacred Pipe to each of the Four Directions, and to the Sky and to the Earth, rotating the pipe between directions. At each position he offered a puff of Prayer Smoke. Completing the ancient ritual, he passed the Pipe to the person at his left shoulder. In turn, each in the Circle stood and repeated the same ritual.

At last the pipe was handed to me. I had been paying particular attention what each person did and was ready for my turn. Standing and receiving the pipe from the person next to me, I faced the center of the circle and held the Pipe reverently. I began the ritual.

Immediately Little Crow rose and stood silent, as a senior circumambulated the inside of the circle, coming to me... politely and respectfully received the pipe from my hands.

I was confused, and more than a bit embarrassed. Mostly I worried that I had done ritual damage to the Pipe Ceremony. The gentleman who had received the Pipe from me politely extinguished the coals in the pipe, cleaned it and, after separating the bowl from the stem, reverently placed it on the leather bag that it lived within.

No words were spoken.

The Circle was broken down, the folding chairs realigned into rows for audience seating. After everyone had been seated, Little Crow took his place before us and delivered a most inspirational message... always beginning the same way, clutching an eagle feather with both hands, saying, "Good morning! I'm Little Crow, clean and sober," acknowledging a time long ago, of substance abuse.

After he had finished his lesson, and the room was prepared for sharing, I approached my friend to offer my apologies for my wrongdoing... although I couldn't for the life of me understand what I had done that had caused the ceremony to end.

My friend took my hands in his, speaking softly – avoiding my eyes as is the tradition not to "steal another's soul" by looking into their eyes. I started to talk and he stopped me with a smile. "Great Elk, you did nothing wrong in your world, however in ours, you stopped the Pipe." I looked at him with a deeply puzzled face, and he continued. "Brother Elk, we do the ceremony following the sun, and when you began to turn the Pipe in the opposite direction, counterclockwise, not clockwise... It broke the power of the ceremony."

I knew instantly what had happened. Nearly every tribe I know does the rituals in a clockwise manner. However, we differ as a Shawnee people. In rotating the Pipe, we do it in a counterclockwise fashion... we are often known as the "contraries." Lesson learned, and our friendship remained unbroken.

Our lives are filled with people who come in and out of our circle, some for long spells and others only briefly. Each in their way shifts our steps upon the Path of Life. Little Crow often would remind us that, "You are created with choice, you have a choice with every breath you take."

Carl Little Crow Bryant was exemplary of those of the Greatest Generation. His life was centered around Choice. Choosing to learn as a child from his elders, Choosing to become a Marine and to serve our nation, Choosing to bug-out when one too many near misses crossed his path, Choosing to correct bad habits early on, Choosing to share his message with anyone who would spend an hour each Sunday morning... my friend Little Crow was the epitome of Choice.

It would do us well to choose who we allow to enter our Circle, to spend time with us. As the old Crusader said in the movie, Raiders of the Lost Ark, "Choose wisely!"

Mitakuye Oyasin, For All Our Relations.

More about this remarkable man: Carl Little Crow Bryant was born in 1933 and raised by Phoebe White-Woman Bryant in Omaha, Nebraska. He joined the Marines at 17, serving for twelve years and, after surviving his third helicopter crash, left the service. For the next several decades, Bryant lived in Orange County, California where he became a professor of American Indian Studies at California State University, Long Beach. At 45, he co-founded, and served as spiritual leader of, the American Indian Church until his retirement in 2003. He was a well-known and respected leader in the American Indian community and was Chaplain of the California Gourd Dance Society. For most of his life he was an "Indian without a Tribe," meaning he had no Federally Recognized Tribal affiliation. In 2002, after a lifetime of leadership for Native Americans he was accepted as a formal member of the Shakopee Mdewakanton Sioux (Dakota) Community in Prior Lake, Minnesota.

- 33 -
Pele Shapes the Sacred Land

The smell of sulfur. Acrid, foreign, almost menacing. Metallic odors, like standing near an ore smelter. Smoke rising from the ground in fumeroles.

Rippling... black rock. Confusing to the eye – shapes like viscous flowing liquid, frozen in place and hard as stone. And hot. The feeling of heat under your shoes as you walk close to recent lava flows.

This is impressive land. Five hundred square miles, two active volcanoes, and an alien landscape unique to this area, the Big Island of Hawai'i, the state's most recently formed island.

And still forming. Pele Honua Mea – she who shapes the sacred land.

The legend of Pele was first told to me when I was five years old. On a family vacation, we took a tour of the Hawai'i Volcanoes National Park. Memorable. Impactful. No words really seem to describe my experience of seeing this land at such a young age. I still remember our tour guide, Kāne, because he told the legends so vividly and engagingly. Perhaps because he was named after one of the four major Hawaiian deities, the giver of life, the creator.

As he drove us through the Park and towards Kilauea, he recited the legend of Pele, the goddess of fire and volcanoes. She is well-known for her passion, jealousy, and power. It is she who lives in the crater of Halema'uma'u.

Pele came to Hawai'i in a canoe from Tahiti. Her sister Namaka drove Pele from their homeland in fear that she would destroy their land with her temper. Going from island to island, the sisters eventually arrived at the Big Island and fought to Pele's death. They say her spirit lives on in all volcanoes but has its home in the

Kane and Kelly
Hilo, Hawai'i

Halema'uma'u crater on Kilauea. When she is angered, she causes eruptions that flow molten rock over the land.

Although these eruptions are unpredictable, violent, and destructive… they also create new land as the lava flows into the Pacific ocean. The island is in a near-constant state of "becoming" due to the two most active volcanoes, Kilauea and Mauna Loa, in the domain of Tūtū Pele (as she is respectfully called by natives – Madame Pele, in other words).

That original trip was haunting and formative for a five year old girl from Ohio. I've kept Kāne's telling of the old legends close to me my entire life. Looking back on it, he was a Wisdom Keeper an elder, passing down the wisdom of his own ancestors to me, the next generation. It was at his suggestion that my mother nicknamed me KiKi.

On a return visit over forty years later, I was fortunate enough to take a helicopter tour of the Park, providing an entirely different perspective than the land tour had done so long ago.

Seeing the lava flows from above impresses upon the viewer its massive influence on the land. The smell of the sulphur, the color of bright red just under the silvery surface of new lava, the steam rising off the ocean as new land is being formed from the flow... It is sobering and inspiring simultaneously.

After all those years, Kāne's voice came back to me as I remembered the mo'olelo (legends) of Tūtū Pele. The perspective from the air brought into clear focus the contrast of destruction and renewal. We saw roads covered in recent lava flow at the same time we were watching new land being formed as the molten rock splashed into the water, cooling it, forming new terrain on the south coast of the island.

Interestingly, in addition to Pele's infamous temper, she is also a goddess of Hula, considered so because it was she who asked her sister Hi'iaka to dance the first hula. Most hula shows even to this day feature the chant *E Pele E Pele* because she is so intricately connected to this native art.

Pele lives on in the mo'olelo of the Kanaka Maoli (the Real People, native Hawaiians). They respect her and fear her equally. Although she may bring destruction, she also brings renewal and the joy expressed in the Hula. It is the contrasting faces of Pele.

We rarely, if ever, can truly see what the future holds. Our lives are a series of victories, defeats, and stalemates. However, when we stop to truly analyze the pattern, we most often see that what, at first, appeared to be a negative, turns into a positive... if we allow and help it to be so. Destruction can give way to a new and better reality.

Sometimes we call such a thing a "blessing in disguise." We lose our job only to find that we have an opportunity for something better, more suited, more profitable. An appointment gets cancelled and then we realize we were needed more somewhere else at that same time. We split from a romantic relationship, get our heart broken, later to find a person far more kind and loving than we imagined possible.

These types of things happen all around us, every day, and we may not always see them for what they truly are. The legend of Madame Pele is the illustration of the concept that when something destructive happens, it usually is paving the way for a new future we had not even dreamed could exist.

The next time you have a stone blocking your path, consider why it might be there. Perhaps you are meant to turn to a different direction, try a new path. Struggling to remove the stone may be a waste of effort. Allow yourself to consider turning away from the stone and towards a new future.

Ha'ina ka inoa no Pele la ea. *(In the name of Pele.)*

- 34 -
My First Shoes

The things we remember, and why they often create a flurry of other thoughts of times long past. Just the other day I was talking with the good people down at the Phoenix Veterans Administration about getting some new diabetic shoes (required attire these days thanks to Agent Orange exposure in Vietnam). The VA for the most part is treating me well, and the shoes they provide me are of a good quality.

I picked up two new pair. To make sure that they fit, I walked across the room, and it brought back memories of a pair of shoes from long ago. A very special pair of shoes.

Clear as day, the memory returned. It was during my first grade in school… in a one room schoolhouse with eight grades, all under the same roof. Just one teacher. That was an amazing year, that imprinted my life in so many ways.

My parents were well educated. Mom a school teacher and English major, and my dad with degrees in medicine and journalism… learning at home before I ever entered into public school was a given. By the age of five, I already knew my "numbers," and the four math disciplines of addition, subtraction, division and multiplication. I could print and write cursive, and read comprehensively well beyond my age. I have been ever thankful that my mother and father encouraged me to always read anything and everything. I became an education sponge early on, and still enjoy "brain stuffing" to this day.

In that one room school house in Sandy Springs, Ohio, each class daily had part of the teacher's attention. I often would eavesdrop on subjects that were being taught to the upper class groups. Brain stuffing, I listened in on geography closely following the teacher as she pointed to where the countries were located on the big map at the front of the room. They chatted about division and multiplication and I followed along on my paper. Things of science fascinated me. Grammar was always a challenge for me because I was thinking of how to say what was in my mind, and not so much about sentence structure... my "one weakness." Topics filled my head with thoughts of adventure, discovery and still excite me today. I remain obsessively interested about nearly everything.

Others have defined me as a modern Renaissance Man. Perhaps. In any case I have been blessed!

But back to the shoes.

On my birthday that spring of my first year in school, I received a gift that I will never forget. A pair of six-eye, lace up, high top shoes from my maternal grandfather. Excitement barely describes the emotion that I had, and can still recall easily.

It was the perfect gift.

They weren't actually the first pair of shoes I ever had. Like most kids in mid-century rural Appalachia, I wore hand me down clothing. A practice driven by necessity, and practicality born by centuries of frugality... "If it ain't broke, don't fix it!"

We were recycling when the term was not defined by modern mores!

These actually were the first shoes that my grandfather Jess Barber ever made for me. They were beyond special.

Grandpa Jess was my mother's dad, and a product of his era. He was born on one of the worse "Dog Days of Summer" in August of 1881. (The summer of 1881 was historic for Ohio in the range and intensity of the heat & drought. It was one of the outstanding weather events in our history. Temperatures reached as high as 111°F with reportedly many deaths from heat stroke.)

He lived nine decades. During his extraordinary life he did everything from being a dirt farmer, baseball player, horse wrangler... and a cobbler. (See other stories about him in this book.)

He made shoes at the Selby Shoe Factory in Portsmouth, Ohio working in many different areas of the factory. From apprentice jobs like "hide'n' and stamp'n" to "upper maker" and "stitcher." As a master cobbler he worked as a "lather, lacer and finisher." Over the years, he grew in the company and was recognized as a most valuable employee.

In those days, in his little workshop at home, he had an area to make and repair shoes for the family... and friends.

That's what people did in those days.

This birthday gift package was in the form of a flour sack tied at the top with a piece of fancy ribbon. The family urged me to guess what was in the package. I guessed several different thoughts, but none were close.

Finally, I was allowed to open my soon-to-be-beloved present. I remember clearly pulling the bow's loose end and watching the cloth fall away. Two shoes, perfect in every way... shiny and new. I held one in my hand and looked at the sole, polished light tan uniformly edged with sturdy stitches. The heel was made of several layers of thick leather. The uppers were laced together with round cord laces evenly crossed over and through six holes punched in the leather. Above the heel at the top of the shoe my grandfather had sewn a leather loop to help pull the boot on. The innards were lined with soft glove leather, and on the inner sole a firm piece of shaped cowhide was stamped two words... "For Jimmie."

I was so beyond proud!

When it was raining or snowing, or just cold, I would be driven to school by one of the family members or a neighbor who was going west. On good days I would walk the three miles to school. I remember wearing my old shoes, although they were worn thin... or even going barefoot on those walks. I would carry my new shoes laced together and tossed over my shoulder. I would sit on the front stoop of the school and put them on before entering the building. I wore them every Sunday to church, carefully polished and shiny.

I loved my shoes! I slept with my shoes. I thanked my grandpa every time I saw him... until, I am sure, he was tired of hearing it. Finally my mom whispered in my ear, "He understands."

As the months passed I regrettably outgrew those shoes. I recall later that brother Mike, almost as appreciative as I was, got them as hand-me-downs. I recall that they were still fresh and sturdy.

And thus, the saga of grandpa's gift, my first pair of new shoes, was complete.

I don't recall where they went after that. They probably went to one of my cousins, and then others, and then others for I am sure they wore well for decades.

There are special gifts we receive that change our lives immeasurably by the receiving of them. But no emotion can compare to the recall of the person or persons who gifted us with such treasures. Treasures stored in the vault with our most prized memories, to be "brought out" to appreciate and reminisce.

Think about those special gifts in your life, and take them out of your vault to enjoy the emotion once more.

- 35 -

She Wore Reindeer Antlers & Played a Djembe

One of my favorite pictures of my sister Helen was taken at a family holiday party in the early 2000s. She is wearing a red turtleneck with a crazy Christmas print vest. She's got felt reindeer antlers with flashing lights on her head, and is banging on a djembe drum with a dear friend of mine... and she has the biggest Helen-grin you ever did see.

Ironically, on the bar right near where she is sitting is a martini glass. I say "ironically" because it isn't hers. Helen never drank alcohol. The picture is so wild and raucous looking, one could imagine she *must* have had a few cocktails. But no...

Helen was high on life. She loved her family, and her life, and her God. She needed no chemical assistance to enjoy loud music and laughter. And her absolute favorite time of the year (second only to Halloween) was Christmas. She was the epitome of a happy child, despite her sixty some years, every time the turn of the calendar brought us to December.

I remember that party well. Several of us were gathered together in the family room because that's where the music was. And, anywhere the music was, that's where you could find both Helen and me. My grand niece and nephew were in there with us, as well as three of my closest friends – one dancing up and down the spiral stairs and making us all howl with laughter, it's a wonder he didn't break his neck that night! I think someone was on a run of playing Bob Seger music, I vaguely recall belting out "Old Time Rock n Roll," while Helen banged on the drum with my friend Ryan and beat out quite a rhythm. (The family room was also where I kept my collection of percussion instruments.)

Helen Herron Hendrix
and Ryan Smith

Despite not meeting her until I was 30 years old (story for another time), Helen was a kindred spirit. She and I hit it off immediately. In fact at that very first meeting, we ended up sitting up talking until the wee hours of the morning – trying to make up for lost time, I imagine.

She was a powerfully passionate woman. She believed what she believed, and she loved who and what she loved... and that was all you needed to know about her. In that way, she was delightfully simple. Not in a derogatory sense of the word, no... in the most wonderful sense of the word. She told you what she thought, she wasn't wishy-washy, you always knew where you stood with her, and she loved with her heart wide open, no mysteries involved.

Like me, she had a temper, and while she wasn't proud of it, she accepted it about herself and strove honestly to be judicial with it. She raised two children with her beloved husband and was one of the most devoted moms I'd ever known other than my own. She embraced her role in her household with pride and a fierce commitment to be the best wife and mom she could be. She railed against coffee klatches and stay-at-home moms that didn't take their responsibility to their homes and families seriously. She did her job as a wife and mom as intently as if she'd been hired into a salaried position. I always admired her for that.

And she was a damn good sister to me for the ten short years I had her. I could talk to her about anything, at any time of the day or night. She was there during my worst times, and my most joyful. I never doubted for one moment how completely she had accepted me, even in our late beginnings of sisterly bond.

Like our father before her, Helen left this world far too soon... and far too abruptly. One morning she was joking with me, and by that night she was gone.

Just. Gone.

Forever.

And she left the way she had prayed to her God that He would allow – quickly and without pain. She was afraid of the actual dying, not what would follow. "Lord, just take me quick," she would say only half-jokingly. "Don't scare me, or rip me into pieces doing it. Just make it quick. I don't want to be scared or hurt."

And He did indeed.

She was the true matriarch of dad's family. I learned later, sadly, that she was the super glue who held us all together and made us toe the family line. When she said we were getting together for a holiday, someone's birthday, or just because, we did it. When she said it was time to draw names for Christmas gift giving, we may have griped a bit because September seemed too early (!)... but we did it.

After she left, things unraveled, but the memories of that decade I was allowed to share with her have remained, and will remain, forever in my heart. Memories and stories to last my lifetime. Some of my silliest moments were spent with her. Side splitting laughter, warm comfort, and a deep feeling of belonging. That was my sister Helen.

I still have the tambourine and reindeer antlers, by the way. And the djembe. I live in the desert now, far away from my Ohio home, but everywhere in our new home, Helen lives in the bits and pieces of her gifts, things she loved, and photos of her smile.

Life is what you make of it.

It is always your choice, and yours alone, whether you smile and laugh, or hold onto pain and sadness. Helen lost our shared dad when she was barely twenty years old and the scar of that pain never left her. And yet she chose to embrace the memories... and to be there for me, to recount the stories of him, so that I could know him also, through her and his family. She shared these things with me with great joy.

Her life was about joy and laughter. When I needed a good side splitter, I knew where to go. She and I would always find some way to get into trouble or mischief. Our sister Diane, tells the same kind of stories – mischief-making silly situations that belonged on I Love Lucy rather than real life.

Helen had her hurts and her challenges, but she taught me that it was ok to laugh in the midst of it, not to take things too seriously because more often that not they would work themselves out in time.

She was right.

Take time to laugh. Take time to be raucous with friends and family. Be joyful. You never know when it may be your last opportunity. Don't waste it.

Put on your reindeer antlers, grab a drum, and live your life as full as you dare.

- 36 -
Hidden Behind the King of Sligo

In the time after the revolutionary war, and the rapid growth of our great new nation, there was still a lot of fear and concern between the original people and these new Americans. Conflicts continued to erupt and there was great distrust on both sides. In the Northwest Territory, thousands upon thousands of young American men, strong of body, and dedicated to "civilize the vast wilderness," had journeyed west to find their fortune. Some came alone, others with family, but all came with the intent of making their Homestead in this wilderness.

It was a heady time for frontier folk as they expanded the American dream.

For the original inhabitants in this vast stretch beyond the Appalachian Mountains, life was much different. As buffalo traces became dirt roads wide enough for oxen pulled wagons, forests were cleared, cabins were built and pastures established... it was evident that their new neighbors were making permanent changes on their ancestral lands.

Many worked hard to get along with these new neighbors, others quietly moved westward beyond the Mississippi, and yet others stood firm to protect their land.

These times were called the Indian Wars and it was a most trying time for everyone concerned. After the War of 1812 and the Indian Removal Act of 1830, most indigenous people had either been forcibly removed west onto reservations, married white folk and established their farms next to the newcomers or, as some did, headed deep in the "hollers" or up the mountains.

No matter which they chose, if they stayed east of the Mississippi, they were subject to removal. When a family was removed, typically their properties would be sold to pay for a military escort who transported them to the reservations. Usually they were only allowed to take a wagon or two with what belongings they could stuff in, and the oxen or horses needed for the journey. Perhaps a cow or a pig.

If they avoided being removed, most assimilated as best they could, assuming European names. "You were always looking over your shoulder, waiting for the strangers with long guns who would be coming to take you way," was the common feeling.

Our Indian family, on my daddy's side, had assimilated well and most strangers would think they were just another "tanned redneck farmer" along the river. We were mixed blood, half breeds, known locally as simply the Waters Family.

As my elders shared, there was an ever present level of paranoia. If the government found they were Indians, surely they would be removed to Oklahoma. That not only applied to the core family, but all the cousins as well. This wasn't an "old wives tale," but a reality.

Because of their Native American heritage, they were not considered "real" Americans... at least not until the 1920s.

(Congress enacted the Indian Citizenship Act in 1924, granting American citizenship to all American indigenous people born in the United States. However, the right to vote was governed by state's law until 1957, and some states barred their right to vote up until then.)

These were real times, with real concerns. Who would want to be rounded up, told to pack a few belongings and move away from your homeland – whose earth contained the dust of your ancestors? This was a constant and perplexing problem.

How could they avoid removal and secure their a future for their children?

As our family's lore goes, someone had learned about a king in Ireland named King Michael Watters. He was the hereditary King of the Island of Sligo where their inhabitants were referred to as "black Irish," descended Celts, who had not been conquered by the Vikings. They were darker, with black hair, brown eyes.

From that description, my elders decided they might just look like Irish. This was based on nothing more than a brief description in the dictionary.

Would this ruse be enough to avoid prying eyes of government officials?

A plan was discussed and all agreed that from that time forward, the native Waters Family would – by the simple act of adding an extra "t" to the name – become Irish Royalty, descendants of the illustrious and mystical King Michael Watters.

Truth be told, we do have a fair amount of Irish heritage, the Duffy's and Gilliland's from the Republic of Ireland and the mostly Scots/Irish McKees from County Ulster, although neither from County Sligo... and nary a drop blood-kinship to King Michael.

But... the illusion was successful.

For two generations, most no one knew that our grandparents had changed the name to protect us.

I shared this with my dad once, when we were sitting near the Shawnee Great House... He was astounded. He had never put the Irish and Shawnee description together.

This is just one of the many stories about how America's First People stayed on their hereditary land. It was not to escape their mass removal to the concentration camps we now call Reservations... it was because of their solemn obligation to care for the graves of the ancestors who had come before them.

We are taught that when the last person forgets where the ancestors are buried, their souls will wander forever, searching for the relatives who had forgotten them.

Like Paul Harvey's, "The Rest of the Story," you would never have known this, if I didn't share it with you.

Make time to visit the gravesites of your ancestors, if you know where they are. If not, locate them. It doesn't matter wether or not you have Indian heritage, what matters is that you are the total sum of all the ancestors who came before you. You might find that you feel an obligation to ensure that they have not been forgotten, that they are still honored.

Responsibility.

Do you feel it?

If so, do what is right.

- 37 -
Grandpa Grew Roses

Grandpa George loved flowers. More specifically, he loved to *grow* flowers. In the spring our tiny front yard had tulips – red, yellow, white, striped, purple, pink, orange – and daffodils too. And then there were the hyacinths. They smelled so wonderful, Grandma Violet used to love to cut them and bring them into the house. The smell was intoxicating.

In the summer, he grew gladiolas, snap dragons, zinnias, dahlias, asters, in every color of the rainbow. The bumble bees spent all summer crawling in and out of the snap dragons, it must have been quite a party for them. There were butterflies, too. So colorful and intricately patterned.

Grandpa George carefully tended all the flowers that grew from bulbs – taking them out of the ground after flowering, storing them in the basement, and then replanting them meticulously. Year after year I watched the rhythm of my grandfather's gardening habit. Our front and back yards went from drab to an explosion of color within weeks. Once we saw the green pushing through the ground at the front of the house, we knew the gardening season had started in earnest and that my grandfather would be out there watching over the progress.

But the pride and joy of my grandfather's flower garden were the roses. There were long stemmed, clusters, white, red, peach, pink, lavender, and yellow. They lined the perimeter of the little patch of lawn we had at the back of our house. He tended to those rose bushes like they were his children. Constantly checking, trimming, pruning. In the fall when the blooms were done, he would carefully cut them all the way back, readying them for the long Ohio winter.

My grandfather was a stoic man. He rarely showed emotion, had a pain tolerance inconceivable to most human beings, and kept his innermost thoughts and feelings to himself. He loved baseball in the summer, football in the fall, and basketball in the winter and spring. He was very opinionated about politics and current events – he read and watched the news a lot. But other than those things... You never knew much what was happening in his head. "Feelings" were not something he ever shared.

But those flowers, those little organic factories that turn sunlight into glucose – he was head over heels about them.

Literally. He had his cushion that he would kneel on, but just as often you'd see him out there bent over in half, butt up in the air, picking out weeds, or just loving his babies.

While he was still working, gardening was the thing he looked forward to doing after work, or on weekends. After he retired, it was his main hobby and he indulged every chance he got quite late into his life. He worked in those flower patches for as long as I could remember.

Eventually, time took its toll and he was no longer able to care for them as he had his entire adult life. Bit by bit, they no longer flowered. Bulbs didn't get planted, and the rose bushes grew out of control until my mother began teaching herself how to care for them.

After he died, my mother moved out of the old house and into suburbia. She brought the rose bushes with her. That is, any of them that had still survived. She lovingly and carefully transplanted them from their longterm home in the city to her new surburban plot south of Cleveland.

She helped them thrive for several years. Alas, the ground was not ideal, hadn't been lovingly tended and fed for as many years as Grandpa had done it. The last of them died a few years later, and we both were really sad. We loved those rose bushes. Having lived with them during all my growing up years, it was sad to think they wouldn't "be" anymore.

As with all things, nothing lasts forever. Not even the roses.

Unbeknownst to me at the time, my grandfather taught me some things about life.

Sadly, there were things he could so easily give to the plants, yet was clearly uncomfortable giving to his human family. That's not to say he didn't feel the same way about us as he did those roses and other flowers. He just wasn't raised to be demonstrative. He surely loved us. He was a reliable worker. He provided for a wife and three girls during and after the Great Depression, and then gladly welcomed his pregnant youngest back to the nest after she was widowed, and his middle child after divorce.

What he could not outwardly show us, he still managed to teach – the patience of planting seeds and nurturing them, and continuing to care for them even after they were full grown. Seeds come in many forms, you know. There are the ones that grow into plants, but there are also the ones that grow into thought and action, characteristics and habits, children and adults.

In my family I learned that no one was without fault, and no one was entirely beyond forgiveness for those faults. We weren't the Brady Bunch. I grew up in an unusual family group (mother, grandparents, and one aunt) but I was very loved. Even by a grandfather who had ideas and ways that were firmly set in stone. He loved us. In his own way. His gardening showed us all a glimpse of a man who cared deeply.

Now in my 50s, I find myself understanding more than ever Grandpa's passion for flowers. There is a sense of accomplishment in watching something grow and mature. Tending to it, feeding it, and enjoying the eruption of color as a reward for commitment and care. It took me moving to the desert, where life is so precious, to appreciate that which was all around me.

I am continually awed at the abundance of plant life and bursts of color, especially in the spring. It is an environment where all that grows has adapted over millennia to exploit every drop of rain – even when they are weeks apart – and to protect itself from the punishing sun, and the spectacular storms of monsoon.

This year I planted six rose bushes of my own. They joined the four jasmine plants I added to the north wall last spring. Scattered around are pots of sun hardy herbs, Spanish lavender, and flowering succulents. This spring I even *bought six hyacinths and will learn how to care for the bulbs, just like grandpa did. I am finding immense satisfaction in the process of tending flowers. They bring me great joy, and now... now I understand my Grandpa George better indeed.*

Grandpa grew roses.

Plant seeds generously, nurture them selflessly, and bask in the joy of seeing them grow into beautiful maturity.

Grandpa George Sabatka
and his beloved flowers

– BONUS SECTION –
Seven Gifts from the Stone of Death

"Each night when we go to sleep, Creator places the Stone of Death on our eyes. When the sun rises the next morning, Creator lifts the stone from our eyes that we might live another day."

This is an old Panji Sippe belief that my Mide' has always taught me: When we open our eyes the next day, it is the gift of Creator which has allowed us to do so.

This morning as I awoke once again to a beautiful blue sky sunny day here in the desert, I was reminded of this gift and several others. Each time Creator lifts the Stone of Death from our eyes, we are given seven gifts to take into our day. These are guideposts that show the path forward, to fulfillment for that day, to peace of mind, and calm for the soul.

Hope – It is the root of all the other gifts, for as long as you have hope, all other things are possible.

Choice – End the feeling of entrapment and become powerful. You are never without choices, they are as limitless as your imagination.

Resources – There is no limit, *we* have no limits. Endless supply is yours for the making, acknowledge your power and create that which you need to take your next steps.

Attitude – It is the driving force of behavior. Stay confident and open to adventures that remind you... you are uniquely you and unforgettable.

Senses – They are your interpretation of the world around you. Through them, you develop a language to communicate your experiences to others. And others use theirs to speak to you.

Action – Choices bring you to actions which bring you to learning and understanding. Take action, follow through, and you will be lead to higher learning.

...and Perfection – We are all perfect and unbroken. Remember it is only your choices or actions which may be imperfect. Alone or together, when we have good strategies, we can accomplish most anything. Accept your perfection and that of others.

Let's begin...

Josefa Cunat Sabatka
& husband Mathew Sabatka

Josefa's Journey
The First Gift – Hope

Josefa Cunat boarded the S.S. Weimar in Bremen, Germany in April of 1891. Alone. She was bound for Ohio in the United States, as documented on the ship's passenger list, where she is said to be eighteen years old. Her "calling" (interesting word) is listed as "servant" and she is assigned to Compartment B in steerage... the compartment in which all unaccompanied single women were given space for the journey to America.

She was born in the ancient town of Písek, South Bohemia, on May 30, 1875.

I have found no record of how she got from her town of Písek, South Bohemia to Bremen, Germany, almost 500 miles away. In the 1890s, travelers were known to make the journey by train or by coach, but some poorer souls actually got there on foot.

Nonetheless, however she got there, she was at the port that spring day. Upon arriving in Bremen, Germany, she would have needed to make her way to Bremerhaven, the port town where all international-bound ships were docked (about 40 mi north of Bremen itself). By the time Josefa made that trip, steam powered tugs pulled barges along the River Weser and the trip took only one day instead of three. Due to steam power, they no longer had to wait for ebb tide to make the final stretch to the docks.

In the 1890s, passage in steerage class from Bremen to Baltimore would have cost around $30 USD – about three weeks of American semi-skilled labor wages at that time.

Josefa's ship for that voyage was the SS Weimar, newly launched that year by Norddeutscher LLoyd. She was a double masted, single screw, steamer approximately 400 ft long and 50 ft wide. Tonnage capacity was nearly 5000 gross tons and could achieve 13 knots of nautical speed (15 mph). It was not a fast journey by today's standards but was certainly more civilized than what would have been the circumstances earlier in the nineteenth century.

On that day in April, Master H. Heineke and crew welcomed aboard over 2400 passengers (1600 of whom were adults), took on over 1800 pieces of baggage (including Josefa's singular piece). He then set course for the North Sea, heading towards the English Channel, and finally out into open seas.

The SS Weimar had three steerage areas "between decks." One for families, one for single men, and one for single women. Baggage was typically stored in an aisle between bunks which lined the outsides of the ship walls. Often, people had to share bunk space with other passengers, taking turns sleeping on wooden plank platforms that served as makeshift beds. It was dark – no portholes – and the smell would have been challenging to say the least. Sea sickness was common, women crying in fear or bereft at leaving homes and families, crowded conditions with no opportunity for proper bathing or hygiene.

Josefa was assigned to Steerage B, the section for single women. There is no indication from the passenger list that she was traveling with anyone. There were Germans, Bohemians, Hungarians, Austrians, Russians... all headed to places in the Midwest. A surprising number had Ohio listed as their final destination, as did Josefa.

During her journey, only two (babies) lost their lives, and one was born in international waters (a baby girl named Marianna Bryczinski), just ten days before the ship made dock in Baltimore.

Josefa arrived in Baltimore on April 22, 1891, exactly 50 years and 2 days before her granddaughter Noreen's birth.

Josefa was my maternal grandfather's mother – my great grandmother.

All during the 1800's and early 1900's, immigrants were leaving their birthplaces to come to America with nothing more than they could carry. Brave people. Desperate people. They were dreaming of a better life.

But the biggest thing they all had in common was **hope**. *Hope that their leap of faith would realize into a new life of safety, prosperity, and robust health. No* *more constant fear of death, no more endless backbreaking work with nothing to call their own, and no more empty bellies as they lay down their heads at night.*

In America... they would lay down their heads on a pillow of hope, with an earnest prayer for honest opportunities. Opportunities they would grasp with outstretched hands, ready to grab hold and never let go.

Hope is the root of every thought, choice, action. Every decision we make begins with the idea to have or be something or someone better than we currently are. Without hope, most of us would lose our lust for life, our reason for being.

Tonight as you set your alarm for tomorrow morning, remember hope springs eternal.

As the Stone of Death is lifted from your eyes for another day... accept the gift of hope.

Recall Josefa's journey, and seize the day with determination! As long as you have hope, anything is possible.

Helen Herron Hendrix
Kelly's 40th Birthday

Don't Sit Down with It
The Second Gift – Choices

"I could hear some woman screaming and I thought, 'Shut up already! Why are you screaming?! It's so loud.' And then I realized later that it had been me. I was laying there in the stairwell trying to figure out what had happened."

My oldest sister Helen was twenty one years older than me. During her short 63 years, she had her share of health challenges. Most significant of which was a fall down the steps leading to her basement when she was in her early forties.

She broke her hip that day. So badly that she needed a full joint replacement.

In today's world, that is almost a nonstarter. They are so common, as are total knees, that they have become routine. Walk in, get a new joint, walk out usually the same day or next, and back to your normal activities within a few short weeks.

Not when Helen fell in 1987. It wasn't like that at all. She was days in the hospital, recovering from both the joint replacement and the fall itself. When she came home, she needed constant care for weeks as she healed and learned to walk again.

She and I were not yet in each other's lives when she broke her hip. (Long story for another time. I was 32 before I met my sisters from Dad's first marriage.) But she told me about it often in following years. And it left her with a chronic pain issue with which she contended the last 20 years of her life.

Shortly after she and I found one another, I was in a significant car crash which left me with trauma induced fibromyalgia. Three years after that, I was diagnosed with rheumatoid arthritis. I spent the next decade fighting my way back from a life of debilitating chronic pain and morbid obesity. By 2011, I had lost 100 pounds, put my RA into remission, and my fibro was just "a thing" in my past.

But during that decade, as I built deep and abiding relationships with my two sisters, Helen and Diane, I was often gifted with Helen's key point of advice, "Don't sit down with it!"

Huh? When she first told me that I laughed.

After some time, though, I came to learn how valuable that advice is. It is filled with complex meaning. The most superficial and basic is... keep moving or your joints will stiffen up and make it that much harder to get moving later. The deepest is... you can choose to let it get you down, or you can choose to acknowledge it and just keep on keeping on.

Choices.

What a novel concept! You mean, I don't have to behave like a broken down old woman in my early 30s? I can choose to acknowledge something but don't give it power?

I still use this diamond of advice to this day. I'm six months out from a total knee replacement and during the entire recovery I had a silent mantra to not allow myself "to sit down with it." At least not for any longer than was necessary to get good sleep and start again the next day.

Every moment of every day we have the privilege to make choices. Our days are filled with them. From the choice to snooze the alarm, to what we wear, what to eat, what to do, with whom to speak, what time to go to bed, and everything in between. Hundreds of choices, every day, are ours to make.

When we experience stress and challenges in our lives, we often say, "But I have no choice!" You may think you do not, and you may be feeling trapped and anxious... but there are always choices. They may not be ones you want to make, they may be uncomfortable and even far from ideal... but they are nonetheless always there.

As the Stone of Death is lifted from your eyes for another day... Accept the gift of choice.

Allow yourself to see options and alternatives. Do not accept the feeling of entrapment and despair. Open yourself to possibilities, both comfortable and safe, and scary and daring.

The **choices** *you are open to, and willing to explore, will bring opportunity and freedom. You are never without choices. Acknowledge it and let it empower you.*

Clara Bonfanti Cannucciari
Great Depression Cooking with Clara

Clara Cannucciari
The Third Gift – Resources

"We had everything in that garden. Saved a lot of money that way. My father planted the garden, then my mother would can everything. So we'd have enough for the winter."

Clara Bonfanti Cannucciari was born in 1915 in Melrose Park, Illinois, on the west side of Chicago. Her Sicilian parents emigrated to America and struggled tremendously when the Great Depression hit. She met her husband Dino while he was touring with the Vatican Choir from Rome in the 1940s. They were married for 43 years. Later she went on to become an unlikely star in a YouTube video series called, "Great Depression Cooking with Clara."

I found Clara's video series online shortly after it became apparent to me that the COVID19 virus was going to have a profoundly negative effect on our economy and on our everyday lives. In the late winter and early spring of 2020, lockdowns were happening all over the US. People were told to stay home unless they needed to go out for medical services or groceries. Vast numbers of service workers lost their jobs and unemployment skyrocketed. Professionals and office workers were allowed to work from home and had to learn how to use Zoom.

Food and other products were becoming a thing to hoard, and were therefore scarce in major supermarkets. At the beginning of March 2020, it looked to me like we should adjust our mentality to one of preparation for rough times ahead. We stocked our food supplies – pantries, freezers, and refrigerators. And we hunkered down to wait it out. We even reduced our use of paper products as much as possible and I began to prepare for how I could stretch our food supply to avoid trips to grocery stores that were not crucial.

And that is when I found Clara on YouTube. At first it was a curiosity to learn what cooking looked like during a time of extreme financial crisis. My own (maternal) grandparents had lived through it in Cleveland, Ohio and raised three girls on the back end of the hard times. They never talked about it, that I can recall, so I never had an opportunity to learn about their experiences first hand.

As the virus continued to decimate large Eastern cities, and the fear started to really take hold, I watched Clara and listened to the stories she told in between her cooking. She had so many hardships to endure with her family, but she speaks about them as just something that happened and they survived, eating "well" – as she confirms again and again – and sticking together as a family.

Even during a time when resources are nearly nonexistent, many people... many Americans... found resources in the most creative and determined way. They made do for food by always cooking at home, growing a large garden for fresh produce with enough extra to "put up for the winter." They darned and repaired clothing repeatedly. And they had imaginative ways to conserve fuel for cooking and staying warm in the Chicago winters.

As the Great Depression lifted... they came out on the other side as a healthy and strong family. Still alive. Still together. Still a family. And stronger than ever to deal with life's sometimes cruel twists and turns.

We all have resources for which we seldom give ourselves credit. We all have the ability to create where there is lack or need. Every one of us is resourceful beyond our wildest dreams. We're simply rarely of the state of mind that we can make things happen. We get stuck in the usual complaints:

"There aren't enough hours in the day!"

"I can't afford that."

"I'm not qualified."

"I've looked everywhere, and I just can't find what I need!"

"I don't know how to do that."

"I just want someone to love and to love me in return!"

Granted, some resources we need for life are indeed limited. Like, time. We have only so many hours in a day and in our lifetime. But…! How we use those hours is the important thing.

Finding resources is not an impossible talent. It is something we all need to learn. Most importantly, it's about setting priorities and understanding that a budget (time, money, your energy) is always necessary to manage limited resources.

And there is always a way to create more – time, money, energy. And we all have the ability to find those ways. We are all resourceful… it is just a matter of acknowledging our own power to be so! Get your mind right, and get creative!

As the Stone of Death is lifted from your eyes for another day… Accept the gift of resources.

Seize this opportunity. Make your day what you want it to be, and supply yourself with what you need to make it happen. Your ability is nearly boundless. Accept it, work with it, and give thanks for it.

Dals-Ed, Sweden

The Escaping Church Mice
The Fourth Gift – Attitude

"Shhh! Shhh!!!! We can't let them hear us! We just need to find our way back out to the car. I think the parking lot is over here somewhere…"

Giggling.

And more giggling.

A teenaged girl and a middle aged woman, creeping through the darkened halls and rooms of a small town church, trying to escape the boredom of the women's luncheon, with its cucumber sandwiches, and twittering gossip.

The more we got lost, the harder we laughed. The more wrong turns we took, the more we had to stifle ourselves. It seemed as though we were caught in a Trojaborg labyrinth.

What would we say if we got caught creeping through the church?

"Wait. No, let's try this door. Now shh! C'mon, follow me. It can't be that far. There has to be a back way out of here. Look, I think I see a stairwell or something!"

And more giggling!

Oh the giggling… And stumbling over furniture. Creaking doors that seemed loud enough they might hear us in Norway! Rooms and halls so dark we could barely see one of us in front of the other.

Eventually we did find our way out to the car. And then we sat there, in Inga Maj's Saab, in that church parking lot, laughing so hard we had tears rolling down our cheeks. What a predicament we'd gotten ourselves into! Again.

During the summers of 1984 and 1985, I spent several weeks in Dals Ed, Sweden with my high school friend Rolf and his mom Inga Maj. That first summer Rolf was working at the Saab plant and so Inga Maj and I were left most days to get into trouble... er, spend time together.

She has always been an adventurous spirit. Even without intention, she would get us – and often her neighbor Rita – into the most hilarious situations. Situations which, thirty five years later, I still recall and retell with guffaws and snorts of delight.

Inga Maj had **attitude**.

There is no other way to describe it. She always made whatever circumstance we'd gotten ourselves into, something fun and memorable. From missing the ferry departure on our way to Denmark and having to make another entire round trip to Sweden and back (see *The Train that Shouldn't Have Become a Ferry* elsewhere in this book)... to midnight drives across the border into Norway with Inga Maj driving me past old abandoned houses and Rita telling me scary stories about them. It was always an experience for the memory book.

Her attitude was one I have admired for all these years. I later found my oldest sister Helen and recognized in her, also, a spirit of fun, excitement, and crazy exploits. The memory of the laughter I have shared with those two women will always be cherished.

Attitude is the driving force behind a person's behavior. Negative attitudes beget negative experiences, responses, and behavior. The opposite is true for positive attitudes.

Attitude can be fleeting or persistent. It is a commentary on both past and present events. When we encounter something or someone more than once, we usually develop an "attitude" about it. Something we like, dislike, something we find distasteful or pleasant. It is determined by ideas, values, perceptions, experiences. Both family life and societal experiences are formative.

In today's vernacular, "attitude" simply means a person who is self-confident, bold, and comfortable in their own skin. Sometimes to a negative extreme.

But, in the case of people like Inga Maj (eighty five and still feisty) and Helen (sadly passed on for over a decade now), it is/was all that... to the positive extreme.

As the Stone of Death is lifted from your eyes for another day... accept the gift of attitude.

Be confident, open to adventures, and explorations of all kinds. You are uniquely you. Never forget it. And rest easy in knowing that others won't either.

Monsoon 2019
Black Mountain Parkway
Cave Creek, AZ

Marvelous Monsoon
The Fifth Gift – Senses

Lightning, bright and yellow, traveling in all directions, in ways I've never seen lightning travel before! Sideways, multiple bolts at once, spider webs of electricity. Thunder crashing so loudly the windows shake. Rain pummeling downward in such quantity and with such force that it looks and feels like all the oceans of Heaven have burst through the clouds at once.

The washes – aka dry river beds – flood almost instantly with runoff from the rains. The ground is so hard and dry, it doesn't allow much to soak in. Instead, it just rolls off mountainsides and down through flat lands, cutting its way through the desert floor in a violent and tumultuous flow over rocks, boulders, and around trees.

Less than 30 minutes ago, the sun was out and we could watch the thunderclouds building higher and higher overhead. Darkening, spreading, moving ever closer. At first we simply watched the lightning from afar, heard the distant rumble. As the storm moved closer, the winds blew themselves into a frenzy, moving dust and grit through the air. Sometimes you can even feel the grit in your teeth, so fine, and foreign in your mouth.

The sense of sudden humidity is unmistakable. You can smell it in the air as it approaches. As the rain actually begins to fall, there is a smell of something like tar... acrid, intense, and thoroughly intoxicating. The chaparral bushes – also called creosote or greasewood – are by far the most distinctive smell in the desert during a rainstorm. It is the smell of something that has been dry as dust, suddenly drenched. The ozone from the intense lightning also fills the air, bringing with it the clean smell of charged ions.

When living in a place where rain is so scarce, there is particular enjoyment feeling the big fat drops of water pelting your skin. They are heavy, and hard hitting – nature's water massage.

During Sonoran Monsoon, all five senses are engaged. We **see** the lightning, **hear** the thunder, **smell** the desert florae, **taste** the grit in our mouth, and feel the **touch** of the raindrops on our skin.

It is one of the most magical times in this beautiful, colorful, and flowering desert my family and I now call home.

As human beings, we process all experiential information (both internal and external) through our five senses. And then we turn them into language!

We all experience things differently, however. For some of us sight is more acute and for others, it is our hearing. Usually one sense is dominant, and for that reason it becomes our language and how we prefer to communicate our experiences to others'.

If one sense or another is lacking, the others will make up the difference. For instance, if someone is blind, their senses of hearing and touch, are likely enhanced. And therefore, their preferred way of communicating may be to tell you about things with references in speech and writing.

As the Stone of Death is lifted from your eyes for another day... Accept the gift of your senses.

They are the gateway to your understanding of the world around you and how you choose to communicate experiences and information to the outside world.

Crossing the Icy Log
The Sixth Gift – Action

Many years back I lived in a lovely place in the middle of the (then) Cuyahoga Valley National Recreational Area – now a National Park. There were trails of every difficulty level, and the CVNRA was my introduction to the joys of hiking.

My initial forays with my hiking buddy were short, flat, trails that could be accomplished in an hour or less. Then I began to venture onto longer, steeper, more challenging trails. Even one night hike where we were rewarded with a coyote serenade under the light of the full moon!

In Ohio, people hike year round. Except for blizzards and drenching rains, you can see people on the trails during just about any month.

One day in the deep of winter, my hiking buddy and I decided we needed to get out for some fresh air. We'd been cooped up in a small apartment for too long, and the smell of the pines was calling to us. We went out to one of our favorite areas to explore a trail we'd not been on past a certain point. The map listed it as a relatively easy hike. The trail wove its way through some old farming land, a hemlock forest, and along a river gorge. We were bundled up in heavy jeans, coats, boots, etc. There was snow on the ground, so we decided an "easy" trail would be most prudent.

We left the car and headed down to the trail head. Down we walked to the creek bed, per the map, and the trail literally disappeared into the creek. The fast... running... creek.

‹squeak!›

A line of stepping stones across the water were barely visible. They were clearly meant to be the path across the water – but they were mostly submerged. Snow had melted recently and the creek was running deep and fast.

‹squeak again!›

That was it for me! I was ready to about face and head on up toward the parking lot. My hiking buddy had to call me back to the creekside.

"Where are you goin'?"

"Back to the car!" ‹duh› "If we can't cross the water, we can't do the trail. What am I missing?" (No one ever accused me of being the most tactful person when I'm disappointed about something.)

"Well! We'll just cross the water. Look, there's a fallen log there. We'll use that to get across."

A feather could have knocked me over at that moment. Fallen log??? No..... **ice covered, slippery, "fallen" log.**

It was then that we had "the discussion" about our next course of **action**. Do we give up and leave? Or do we attempt to cross the water. You already know what my choice was. But "the hiking buddy" was dead set on pressing onward.

I'd never attempted such a thing. All I could think of was high school gym class where, as ‹ahem!› a plump teenager, I could barely "scooch" my way across a balance beam. It was 1998, and at 32, I was still quite plump and just couldn't imagine myself "scooching" on ice, over quickly running icy water. It seemed, to be frank... stupid. Wreckless. Nonsensical. Insane.

But he did have a way of making anything sound possible and even excitingly adventurous. So... I stood on the bank watching how he did it – all 6'6" of him with long arms and legs. He made it look perfectly doable, and not nearly as scary as my first impression.

Before I knew it, he was on the other side, smiling and laughing and encouraging me to come over.

Uh huh.

Onto the log I scrambled. My fat short little "herron legs" (as my family calls them with such irony) hanging off either side of a log that suddenly felt waaaaay thicker than it looked. I felt like I was splayed in two. And now I realized I had nothing - no thing - to hold onto other than the damnable ice covered log.

"The Icy Stream"

Right-o.

I reached in front me and down to the log – per the instructions shouted to me from "the other side" – and began the attempt to pull myself along, inch by inch. The seat of my jeans was already soaked from the melting ice. I moved as a sloth on a hot humid jungle day.

Except I wasn't in the jungle and, thankfully, I was right side up.

Yet all the same, I was on an ice covered log, in an Ohio forest, praying to all the gods that were, to please please please not let me fall into the rushing water below.

It was touch and go, literally, for the fifteen minutes or so it took me to actually get to the end of the log. At one point there was a... knot... in the log, over which I had to move without skewering myself.

Eventually, I made it. But you knew that, right? I'm a pretty determined person once I get started on something. "Persistent" they call me these days.

Yes, I made it. My butt wet and cold, my boots soaked because I had to step in the water to get off the damn log. But... I made it.

Laughing. Squealing. Breathing hard.

What a rush! I did it! And I didn't die!

On the hike we went. I never did really dry off until we got home but the rush of that fifteen minutes spent crossing the icy log has stayed with me all these years.

I made the decision to stop agonizing and just take **action**. *And that is precisely what led me to the conclusion of, "Laughing. Squealing. Breathing hard. What a rush! I did it! And I didn't die!"*

Sure, I could have fallen in, and been gravely injured or worse. But I didn't. I trusted the person with me, but most of all, I trusted myself to take that action.

In a previous section, we discussed **choices**. *We all make the best choices we can at the time, and usually it is to* **act** *in some way. To do something. All actions have a purpose and a positive intention, and through our actions, we begin to understand. We engage, and we practice. And we learn.*

As the Stone of Death is lifted from your eyes for another day... Accept the gift of action.

Make your choices, and then take action on them. What you do will bring you to the next step of your learning. How you act will determine your next choice, and your next action, and so on.

Nothing can stand in your way unless you choose to take no action. Keep on, keepin' on.

The Eagle and the Pine Tree
The Seventh Gift – Perfection

In the time before time – long before there were two leggeds – there were the finned people, winged people, and four leggeds. All creatures went about their lives, swimming though the oceans and rivers, flying over beautiful Turtle Island, and roaming the bountiful forests and plains. Life was very good. Bellies were always full, and everyone had enough of everything they needed to be happy.

And they were very very happy. They were so happy that they began talking with one another about how to express their gratitude to Creator.

Many ideas were proffered but it was agreed the Pine Tree had the best idea. Pine Tree was the tallest tree in the land. His branches soared towards the heavens.

"My trunk is tallest and I will grow even more branches that will reach up to brush the face of Creator and express our Joy and Gratitude for everything He has gifted us."

All agreed this was a great idea!

So Pine Tree grew and stretched... and gre-e-e-ew and stre-e-e-etched. He reached as far as he could reach and still, he could not come close to touching Creator.

"I should do it," cried Eagle. "I will fly up into the sky, high enough to touch Creator's face and share our feelings!"

Eagle flew higher, and higher, and higher still. She flapped her wings harder than she ever had... and still, she could not come close to touching Creator.

She came back, exhausted, out of breath, and ashamed of her failure. Everyone was sad and despondent.

"How will we ever let Creator know how happy and grateful we are? He must know. He has been so generous with us."

Original artwork by Jim Great Elk Waters

They talked and talked until finally Pine Tree looked at Eagle and said, "If you go high up into my tallest branches, you can begin your journey from there and certainly you will be able to reach Creator then! We will work together to bring the message of the People to Creator!"

Everyone perked up and clapped and cheered. "Yay! Pine Tree & Eagle will deliver our thanks!"

So Eagle flew up to a branch of Pine Tree, and there she rested. Again, she flew up, this time to a higher branch still. And she rested. She repeated this until she got to the very topmost branches of Pine Tree's tall grandeur.

From there she could see all across the Land. The beautiful mountains and valleys, crystal clear rivers and streams, deep blue seas and oceans. What a gift they had been given! It was breathtaking indeed.

With a renewed sense of obligation and energy, she soared even higher. Before long, she had flown high enough. She gently brushed Creator's face, sharing the People's gratitude through her wing feathers and the cry of the Eagle.

Creator understood and was so very proud of them.

Afterwards she flew back down to the Land, and told everyone of her adventure – what she'd seen on the journey, and how she had delivered their Message.

They were enthralled with the tale and celebrated well into the night, honoring Pine Tree and Eagle for working so well together.

Everything Creator has ever made is perfection. And, from that point forward, they knew always that their individual perfection could create compounded perfection when they worked together to accomplish a singular goal.

Not one of us is broken. Creator is perfection, and therefore brings forth perfection in all things.

Sometimes we are disappointed in ourselves and come to believe we cannot accomplish our dreams. At worst, we give up. At best, we acknowledge there are only bad choices and strategies, not bad or broken people.

When we combine our own perfection with others', and an excellent strategy... we can accomplish amazing feats.

As the Stone of Death is lifted from your eyes for another day... Accept the gift of perfection.

Your own. Others'. And all of Creation.

Don't doubt it. Don't fight it. **Be** *it.*

The Lesson...

Now I have shared with you the story of the Stone of Death and of the Seven Gifts we receive each day the stone is lifted.

These gifts all have their roots in the Four Stepping Stones of Life – Fear, Time, Joy, and Vision. We must remind ourselves every day that to be, do, and have everything we need *and* desire (for they are not the same thing), these seven concepts are guides to success.

Hope – It is the root of all the other gifts, for as long as you have hope, all other things are possible.

Choice – End the feeling of entrapment and become powerful. You are never without choices, they are as limitless as your imagination.

Resources – There is no limit, *we* have no limits. Endless supply is yours for the making, acknowledge your power and create that which you need to take your next steps.

Attitude – It is the driving force of behavior. Stay confident and open to adventures that remind you... you are uniquely you and unforgettable.

Senses – They are your interpretation of the world around you. Through them, you develop a language to communicate your experiences to others. And others use theirs to speak to you.

Action – Choices bring you to actions which bring you to learning and understanding. Take action, follow through, and you will be lead to higher learning.

...and **Perfection** – We are all perfect and unbroken. Remember it is only your choices or actions which may be imperfect. Alone or together, when we have good strategies, we can accomplish most anything. Accept your perfection and that of others.

Adean. (It is done.)

James Arthur Watters, Sr.
Jim's dad

Conclusion

As it was in the beginning, so may it end.

The inspiration for this book came from our Elders, stories learned from them, and our own muddling-through-life recollections. Now that you have read it all, we hope you are equally inspired, amused, and feeling good about life.

We are all children, created from dust and earth, and to the same we all shall return. Along the way, we experience, learn, and grow. Sometimes it's rough going, others it's blissfully easy. But through it all we gather our own Wisdom and, through good charity, do our best to instill our learning to those coming after us.

"Family" is an interesting thing... you can't choose 'em, sometimes you want to run from 'em, but in the end, they are the solid foundation of each of us.

Every family has stories galore. Crazy ones, funny ones, sad ones, amazing ones. Together they weave the fabric of our lives – denim, satin, dungarees, and lace. Threads holding us together in a way that makes us stronger than the individual pieces.

We've told you ours... now you tell yours. Keep the memories and the life lessons alive for the coming generations. What laughter can you share, what poignant memories, what rallying cry?

Do not go gentle into that good night. Go with a loud and proud voice. Tell the stories, show the photos, keep the lessons – and your Elders – alive.

Be well...

Left to Right: Noreen, Kelly, Violet, Marlene
Three generations of Sabatka girls.

Cast of Characters, Places and Interesting Things

Adean – Mide' term for "amen." Literally, it translates to "It is done." It is often used at the end of prayers and ceremony.

Aunt "Lil" Lillian Book – Drew Book's wife.

Aunt Cora and Uncle Floyd Munn – Jim's dad's aunt and her husband Floyd. She was one of the renowned Price Girls and was best known for her delectable pound cake.

Aunt Marlene Sabatka – Kelly's mom's sister, middle child of the three girls born to George and Rose Violet Sabatka.

Aunt Ruth and Uncle Fred Brown – Jim's mom's sister and her husband. Successful entrepreneurs.

Auroro Borealis – aka The Northern Lights. Light display in the northern latitudes caused by disturbances in the Earth's magnetosphere.

Baba (Helen Rericha) – Kelly's husband's maternal grandmother. First generation American born Czechoslovakian, raised on a farm in Ohio's coal mining country, mother to two girls Dolores and Virginia.

Big Dad – Jim's dad's father, George Thomas Watters IV.

Bohemia – a region in western Czechoslovakia, formerly a duchy of Moravia, also where Prague (Czech capital) is located.

Boston Tea Party – The colonist's nighttime raid on the tea stored in Boston, dumping the bales of tea in the harbor was to protest the 1773 British Tea Act, created to prop up the failing East India Company by making it the sole seller of the American tea trade.

Brör – Rolf's uncle who owned a lakeside cabin in Dalsland, Sweden.

Bryan Pavlovic – Kelly's husband.

Buena Vista – An Ohio River town in south west Scioto County, Ohio. It was founded in the early 1800's for the corporate headquarters of the Buena Vista Store Company.

Caesar's Palace – famous casino and resort in Las Vegas, Nevada.

Cedar Point Amusement Park – large amusement park in Sandusky, Ohio, on Lake Erie, and a regular summer spot for day trips as Kelly was growing up and into adulthood.

Clara Cannucciari – Unlikely YouTube "star." Born in 1915 in Melrose Park, Illinois, on the west side of Chicago. Her Sicilian parents emigrated to America and struggled tremendously when the Great Depression hit. She met her husband Dino while he was touring with the Vatican Choir from Rome in the 1940s. They were married for 43 years. Later she went on to become an unlikely star in a YouTube video series called, "Great Depression Cooking with Clara."

Copenhagen – capital of Denmark.

Cuyahoga Valley National Park – formerly "National Recreation Area." The park lies along the Cuyahoga River between the Ohio cities of Cleveland and Akron. The Ohio and Erie Canal Towpath Trail is a restored section of the canal's original towpath. In the park's north, the Canal Exploration Center details the 19th-century waterway's history. Towering Brandywine Falls is one of several waterfalls. The Cuyahoga Valley Scenic Railroad runs through the park.

Dals-Ed – Small rural town in Sweden where Kelly spent the summers of 1984-1985 with Rolf and his mom Inga Maj.

Diane Herron Blankenship – Kelly's second oldest half sister, they share dad Cliff. Still living, in rural West Virginia.

Drew Book – Jim's cousin Andrew J. "Drew" Book who was a nationally renowned primitive artist.

Ford Ferguson tractor – The tractor Jim's grandfather Jess Barber bought to farm on Lower Twin.

George Sabatka – Kelly's mom's dad. First generation American born Czechoslovakian. Avid flower gardener.

Gertie Barber (Ma Gertie) – Jim's mother's mom.

Grandmother Earth – The name that many North American First People use to refer to the earth. Where all seed is grown within.

Grandfather Sky – The name that many North American First People us to refer to the sky, where the seed is nourished with sun and rain.

Great House (Chìsakewin Wicon) – Refers to the central house of worship of the Shawnee and other Eastern Woodland Native Peoples.

Greatest Generation – The generation that came of age during the Great Depression and fought in World War II. Its name came from the book The Greatest Generation by Tom Brokaw, a journalist for NBC.

Helen Herron Hendrix – Kelly's oldest half sister, they shared dad Cliff. Passed away in 2009.

Helsingborg/Helsingør – sister town in Sweden and Denmark, respectively, on the north and south shores of the Øresund, the strait that separates Sweden from Denmark.

Hồ Chí Minh (Nguyễn Sinh Cung) – born in 1890. From 1919 to 1923, Thành (Ho) while living in France, was influenced by the Socialist Party of France and embraced Communism. Thành (Ho) returned to Vietnam to lead the Việt Minh independence movement. Ho became president (1945-1969) the Democratic Republic of Vietnam (North Vietnam). He was the leader of the Vietnamese nationalist movement for nearly three decades.

Inga Maj Nilsson – Rolf's mom, native and resident in rural Sweden, language teacher.

Jess Barber – Jim's mother's dad.

Jim's Dad – James Arthur Watters, Sr.; aka: Chief Ten Moons (*Okema Metathwe Dekeelswa*).

Jim's Mom – Nelle Fitch (Barber) Watters.

Jimmie's Place – (1920's-1960's) George T. and Jessie Watters created a Mecca for travelers on US 52 featuring good food and comfortable clean lodging. They built a business in Sandy Springs (Adams Co.) consisting of a restaurant, tourist cabins and Gulf gas service.

Josefa Cunat Sabatka – Kelly's maternal grandfather's mother (great grandmother). Born in Pisek, South Bohemia, she journeyed to America alone, at the age of seventeen.

Kelly's Dad – Clifford Herron, dead of a heart attack at age 45. A native of West Virginia coal mining country, welder by trade.

Kelly's Mom – Noreen Sabatka Herron, a career RN, widowed at 25 while she was pregnant with Kelly.

Kiddie Park – an 11-ride amusement park located in Brooklyn, Ohio, designed specifically for children and families. Memphis Kiddie Park opened on May 28, 1952 and is still operational as of 2020. It is the home to the oldest running steel rollercoaster in America, the Little Dipper.

Kümmel – a sweet, colorless liqueur flavored with caraway seed, cumin, and fennel. According to some historians, kümmel liqueur was first distilled in the Netherlands during the late 16th century by Lucas Bols.

Lower Twin Creek – One of two post glacial creeks in western Scioto, County, Ohio that empty into the Ohio River.

Ma Jessie – Jim's dad's mother, Jessie Ada Lucretia (Price) Watters. One of the renowned Price Girls. Best known as Mrs. Santa Claus to her neighbors.

Monsoon – In the Sonoran Desert, it is the period of mid to late summer called "wet summer." Known for torrential rain, high winds, and incredible lightning storms. It renews the desert flora and fauna each summer.

Mide'wiian – (Algonquian) Mide' Way, Panji Seepe Naube pre-columbian traditional religion, similar to the Anishinaabeg (Ojibwe) Midewiwin teachings

Mr. Francis – Jim's Next door in Buena Vista.

Mr. Miller's General Store – one of two general stores in Buena Vista in the 1940's and 50's.

Mrs. Tinker – Child psychologist at University Hospital in the 1970s whom Kelly saw as a child to help with her severe separation anxiety.

Nonat – Czechoslovakian brand of "Ichthammol." aka, black salve or drawing salve. It is used to draw out splinters,, boils, bee stings, etc.

Ol'Jack – Jess Barber's mule on Lower Twin Creek.

Panji Seepe Naube – (Algonquian) meaning Blue Creek People, and refers to the extended familial group of pre-history mound builder people (possibly Ft. Ancient Culture) who joined the Shawnee confederacy cica 1400's.

Pele – Hawaii'an goddess of fire, volcanoes, and hula. Legend says she lives in the the crater of Halema'uma'u on Kilauea, in the Hawai'i Volcanoes National Park on the Big Island of Hawai'i.

Pissen Katten – Rolf and Inga Maj's tabby cat during the mid 1980s.

Pol Pot (Saloth Sar) – born in 1925 . He was a Marxist trained political leader whose communist Khmer Rouge government in Cambodia (1975-1979) where an estimated 1.5 to 2 million Cambodians died of overwork, starvation and execution. Pol Pot's regime was one of the most barbaric in recorded history.

Puddenhead – Jim's Cousin George T. Watters V, US Marine who served with distinction in the South Pacific, during World War II.

Red Fox – Chief Red Fox Knox, Ohio Shawnee Village Chief.

Rolf Andersson – Dear friend to Kelly since 1981. Native and still a current resident of Dalsland, Sweden, language teacher in the small town of Bengtsfors.

Sachem – Head Chief among the Algonquians or other tribes of the northeast. The Anishinaabe called them ogimaa, and the Algonquin, ogimà... all having the same meaning.

Sake – Japanese rice wine.

Slavic Village – The small, very ethnic, neighborhood of Cleveland, Ohio, where Kelly was born and raised in an 800 sq ft home with her maternal grandparents, mom, and one aunt, Marlene.

Spaylaywitheepi – (Algonquian), the Ohio River, one of the five major waterways in the United States.

Stone quarry – Buena Vista Store Company (1814 through the turn of the 1900's) sourced materials on the bluffs above the Ohio River and the Little Vastine Creek, Buena Vista, Ohio. Buena Vista sandstone, quarried from sandy layers of the Cuyahoga Formation in the Portsmouth region, in Adams and Scioto Counties, near the Ohio River, was one of the earlier types of stone sent to Cincinnati by river. This stone was also referred to simply as freestone.

The Dakota – two of the three main divisions of the Sioux, the Eastern Dakota and the Western Dakota.

The Olympia – A popular theater in the old ethnic neighborhood of 55th Street and Broadway in Cleveland, Ohio. It opened in 1913 as a vaudeville venue and closed in 1980 after being used as a movie theater for many years.

Tonette Venturino-Howbert – Jim's cousin.

Tram Road – the road from the top of the bluffs above Buena Vista that was used to haul the Freestone to the Ohio River, to be used in building up and down the river.

Vernors – a brand of ginger soda popular in the midwest United States. It has a flavor unique from ginger *ale* and is used in some families for nausea.

Violet Rose Machovec Sabatka – Kelly's mom's mom. Second generation American born Czechoslovakian. Helped raise Kelly after her dad died, and still spoke many words in her native tongue. Kelly continues to use them to this day, holding her ties to her Eastern European roots.

Women's Council – refers to the Shawnee tribal women's leadership group.

Kelly Violet Herron Pavlovic
Jim Great Elk Waters

About the Authors

Elder, Shawano Mide' Pa-we'wa Jim Great Elk Waters, brings a most unique presence. For over 800 moons as a traveler in this Place and Time, Great Elk has been imbued with a priceless collection of wisdom and knowledge. He is descended of the Panji Seppe People of Ohio, the Shawnee/Pekowi Sachem Straight Tail and is also proud of his Scots Irish, Scandinavian, German, and Sephardic Jewish ancestors.

Kelly Violet (Talking Heron) Pavlovic traces her ancestry all over the globe. She has genetic ties to Eastern Europe, the British Isles, Africa, and Ashkenazic/Sephardic Jewish culture. She is also a descendent of Hathawekela Shawnee Chief Walking Panther Longtail.

They are both practitioners of the ancient Mide'wiian Native American Faith. Elder Great Elk and mShemah Talking Heron are both Fourth Order Mide'.

They humbly offer a living repository of Traditional Wisdom from their collective tribes... The Ancestors.

Together, as professional speakers and authors, they share the Wisdom of their Ancestors and forever transform audiences around the world.

MORE FROM JIM & KELLY

View from the Medicine Lodge
A Modern Perspective on Ancient Wisdom

In this collection of essays, stories, and poems, your guides open the Medicine Lodge, and the wisdom found within, recounting their encounters on life's path – from the beautiful to the mundane. With this insight, you will look to the far horizon of the Turtle Island, and deep within... to the center of your soul."Since Creator first made two-leggeds, humans have searched for their soul and its relationship with all things. From the sacred confines of the Medicine Lodge you will gain perspective, and learn to Walk in Balance within your center, with all Creator's Creations."

Quiet Moments Series

Quiet Autumn Moments
Wisdom of the Ancients to Harvest Your Growth

Quiet Winter Moments
Wisdom of the Ancients to Warm Your Days

The ideal daily focal point to energize and enlighten your spirit with insights rooted in Ancient Wisdom, written for the contemporary reader. The authors were inspired, for they knew this sage wisdom would change lives. By our Elders spoken word and their traditions observed, they are the genesis for this book. There is no wrong way to use this book, it is all about you!

The Keepers' Kitchen
Food that Nourishes Body & Soul

A collection of delicious – and good-for-you – recipes from our kitchen to yours. Learn how to make the tastiest use of whole ingredients while keeping it simple and quick. We love to cook and to share food with family and friends. This is a work of love and a small sampling of dishes we prepare regularly. Our sincerest hope is that you experiment, have fun, and enjoy them all. We've also included some notes on what we like to keep in our pantry for healthful, scrumptious, meal prep. Eat well!

Julia Kasik Machovec
Kelly's mom's grandmother

NOTES

Baby Jim with parents
Jim and Nelle Watters

www.ingramcontent.com/pod-product-compliance
Lightning Source LLC
Chambersburg PA
CBHW071813080526
44589CB00012B/777